Butter
Side

Up

Butter Side Up

*How I Survived
My Most Terrible Year
& Created My
Super Awesome Life*

JANE ENRIGHT

swp

SHE WRITES PRESS

Published 2022
Printed in the United States of America
Print ISBN: 978-1-64742-075-8
E-ISBN: 978-1-64742-076-5
Library of Congress Control Number: 2022901398

For information, address:
She Writes Press
1569 Solano Ave #546
Berkeley, CA 94707

Cover and interior design by Tabitha Lahr

She Writes Press is a division of SparkPoint Studio, LLC.

Photo © Rich Vintage Photography

Contents

....

For:
Clayton, for giving me encouragement and strength
Jenn, for sharing true friendship and joy
My father, for sharing the gift of humor
Buddy, for staying by my side

and

Mom, Rob, Ross, and Ryan for sharing
their unconditional love and believing in me.

Prologue

....

I never had a slice of bread,
Particularly large and wide,
That did not fall upon the floor,
And always on the buttered side!

—JAMES PAYN

The question of why a piece of falling toast tends to land butter-side down more often than butter-side up has plagued the human mind for centuries.[1] Dropped toast is a universal example of our tendency as individuals to view the world more negatively than positively—commonly known as "Murphy's Law". We favour believing whatever can go wrong, will go wrong over a more optimistic viewpoint.[2]

For some, the outcome of dropped toast can make the difference between having a good day or a bad one. For instance, you know it is going to be a good day when your toast lands butter-side up; that's because butter-side up can be salvaged. However, if your toast lands butter-side down, you need to start from scratch.

---

1. Wikipedia.org/butteredtoastphenomenon
2. Matthews, R.A.J. (1995). "Tumbling toast, Murphy's Law and the fundamental constants". *European Journal of Physics.* 16 (4): 172–176.

Tumbling toast can also be a metaphor for change. In the blink of an eye, the unexpected can happen. Your life can suddenly be toast—butter-side down, full of icky stuff you don't want anywhere near you. Conversely, you can land butter-side up with possibilities you could never have imagined. Consequently, life puts all of us through change. One might even say life is change.

This begs the question: When the unexpected occurs, how do we successfully navigate change so we can move forward, not backward; make our ideas happen; and land butter-side up in the game of life?

Introduction

....

"The first step to getting somewhere is to decide that you are not going to stay where you are."
—J.P. MORGAN

There are essentially two kinds of change: planned and unplanned.

Planned change is a conscious choice or decision. This might include taking a trip, planning to have children, changing your career, moving house, getting your driver's licence, or deciding to lay off the pizza and bulk up on kale salads.

Unplanned change is an unexpected event or consequence of a circumstance. This may include illness, accidents, a layoff, a divorce, or a pandemic. The reality is that life puts all of us through unplanned change—you know, *stuff*. Unplanned change can lead to grief, depression, stagnation, indecision, or sadness, and make us question everything we once thought we knew for sure. On the flip side, unexpected change can also open doors; bring us joy, happiness, and excitement; offer new opportunities and experiences; usher in new love and friendships; and build faith, hope, strength, and courage we never knew we had.

I am an ordinary person. I have also been through, and survived, some extraordinary, life-changing events and have come out the other end better than I was before. My life has not always been super-awesome. Some of my experiences, many beyond my control, have been super-awful, pushing me to limits I did not know were possible. This includes enduring and surviving three life-altering, uncontrollable events and losing everything in the span of twelve months. Throughout it all, I was able to look at the lighter side of life and understand that embracing change, staying positive, and having faith are the difference between having a super-rotten life and a super-awesome one.

This book is not about self-help jargon. It is edutainment for the soul. My goal is to inspire and encourage you—with a healthy dose of humour along the way—to successfully navigate change so you can move forward, not backward; make your ideas happen; and create the new and improved storyline of *your* super-awesome life. Over the course of this book, I'll show you how to . . .

- Find clarity of thought so you can find answers when you need them
- Develop courage to handle things when they are upside down
- Learn to advocate for yourself and others in difficult situations
- Build strength to help you hold on when all you want to do is let go, and let go when all you want to do is hold on
- Create strategies and know-how to successfully maneuver change in your life

Along the way, I'll share stories and ideas to help you find balance and fun, and encourage you to believe in yourself so you can move forward, make your ideas happen, and land butter-side up in the game of life.

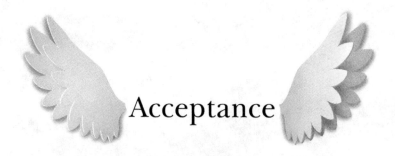

Acceptance

CHAPTER ONE

Why Does My Head Hurt So Much?

....

*"Nothing is so painful to the human mind
as great and sudden change."*
—MARY WOLLSTONECRAFT

"Everyone is so nice here. I can't remember who anyone is, but you're the nicest and the prettiest."

I've just arrived at the ICU step-down unit before morning rounds. I'm in room fourteen, the one closest to the nursing station, the one with a window.

I smile warmly. "I was here yesterday. How are you feeling?"

Mr. C was transferred from emergency and has been hospitalized for almost ten days. I take his hand. His arm is swollen and blue, hopefully from unsuccessful IV attempts and not sepsis. His blood pressure is stable but just barely.

"I have such a headache. My head hurts so much. Why do I have such a headache?"

He has kind, twinkly-blue eyes, a warm smile, and a PhD from a very prestigious business school. On top of that, he is a full-tenured professor and CEO of his own research firm.

Mr. C's head hurts so much because he experienced two traumatic brain injuries within a forty-eight-hour period. Ten days ago, he was in a car accident, which, unbeknownst to him, caused a small bleed in the front temporal region of his brain when his head hit the steering wheel. Fourteen hours later, Mr. C fell backwards from a standing position onto the concrete cement floor in his garage. The fall caused his brain to ricochet to the left, then right, with severe bleeding on both sides.

To add insult to injury, he also has a fractured skull just above his brainstem. Had that fracture been a millimetre to the left, Mr. C would be on a ventilator. Now, despite all this trauma, Mr. C is full of questions.

I look at the vitals monitor; his heart rate is still irregular, and he is hypertensive again. The doctor on call last night decided to suddenly cut Mr. C's pain meds. With this type of injury, they don't like to sedate a patient too much. The result is crushing headaches.

"Are you a nurse?"

Mr. C doesn't know it yet, but today is going to be a tough day. Quite frankly, if it were up to me right now, I would hand him a forty-ouncer of scotch and an Egg McMuffin for breakfast, and let the day happen. For a moment I ponder whether or not to spill the beans.

After what seems like an eternity, I gently brush back his hair, stroke his stubbled cheek, and say, "No, I'm not a nurse. You're Clayton, but sometimes I call you C. I'm Jane, but sometimes you call me J. We live together. We're engaged. I'm your partner.

> Sudden, unexpected change can
> occur rapidly, at any moment.

4

....

Dear friends and family,

I am writing to share that unfortunately, C has suffered a very serious head injury.

Doctors think he may have suffered a seizure, which triggered a subsequent serious fall in the garage this morning.

I found him semi-conscious and bleeding and called 911; he was taken by ambulance to hospital. He has a fractured skull and a significant bleed in his brain, which may require surgery to fix.

We don't know exactly what happened because he can't tell us. He is non-verbal and altered, and there is significant damage to the car, which cannot be explained. It suggests he may have had a car accident sometime beforehand.

He is on anti-seizure meds and is being closely monitored by the neurology team. He is receiving excellent care, and the nurses and doctors are fantastic. He will be given a number of CT scans to monitor any changes. We will know better how things will shape up over the next few days and if he requires surgery.

Please forgive my email rather than a call. It is a very emotional time, and I thought this would be the best way to reach out to everyone who cares about C to let you know what has happened.

Please keep us in your prayers, and I promise to provide updates as I receive them.

Love to all . . .

Jane

....

CHAPTER TWO

The Upside of Erased Is . . .

"Everything can change at any moment,
suddenly and forever."

—PAUL AUSTEN

"I live with you? We live together?"
"Yes, we live together."
"How old are you?"
"I'm fifty-one."
"How old am I?"
I tell him that, too.
"Do we sleep together?"
"Yes, we sleep together."
He pauses. "Do our parents know?"
"That we live together, or that we sleep together?"
"That we sleep together."
"Yes, my parents know, but your parents are deceased."
Behind those kind, tired, pained eyes is a look of wonder, amazement, and downright astonishment. There is astonishment and amazement on my face, too; first, because this is the

most conversation Clayton and I have had since his accident; and second, because I am slowly coming to the realization that after ten days in the hospital, Clayton still does not know who I am and may never know who I am—ever.

If you were reading about this in a textbook, this part of the change process would be entitled "Moving Towards Acceptance."

"Where do we live?"

I fumble with my iPhone to look for a picture of the house. "We live here," I say, pointing at a lovely four-bedroom home. "We've lived here together for six years."

I scroll through the pictures of rooms in the house, watching him, hoping for a glimmer of remembrance . . . or something. He eagerly looks at each picture, silently. I talk about our home, our travels together around the world, children, friends, but there is no recognition, no memory of Clayton and me, period. Like a Zamboni clearing an ice rink, in one fell swoop, our life together has been, in a word, erased.

Finally, something comes out—not a memory, but something totally unexpected.

"Wow, I live with you, and we live there. I must be a lucky son of a bitch!"

Now, most people coming out of a semi-coma and realizing that they cannot remember anything about the past six years, let alone their partner, might be distraught, sad, or angry. Not Clayton; he was anything but those things. He was enthusiastic and grateful about his life. In fact, it seemed he had totally skipped the denial part in the change process and gone straight to acceptance—or so I thought.

Acceptance is the first step towards successfully navigating change of any kind, especially rapid, unexpected change. When change happens, our tendency is to push it away, resist, or deny it. Accepting that change has occurred does not mean you have to like what is happening. Rather, it is the actual willingness to accept change, not resist or deny it, that helps you move forward and shift your perspective towards a more positive mindset.

Unfortunately, this was neither my, nor Clayton's first rodeo with head trauma.

Clayton and I had come to live together six years before, after his first accident. We were dating and he had been visiting me for the weekend along with my parents, who were in town from the West Coast. Clayton went for a bike ride, flew over the handlebars, and landed on his head. Thankfully, he had a bicycle helmet on, but he was knocked unconscious for forty-five minutes, required surgery on his hand, and suffered a small (nothing like this one) bleed in his brain that left him unable to work or drive for many months. Because of his injuries, he could not live by himself. His home at that juncture was hundreds of kilometres away. Consequently, when I arrived at the emergency room the first time, the attending physician looked at me and said, "Can he stay with you?"

Unfortunately, my luck with head injuries was not much better. In 2017, I suffered a life-altering concussion when I was hit fiercely in the head with a volleyball at my son's tournament. It happened during a warm-up at the provincial championships. I was in the designated seating area, waiting to score the game. I never saw the ball coming towards me or knew where it came from, and neither did my son.

Unbeknownst to us, a participant had drilled the ball into the stands—not to hit me, per se, but because he was angry. The player who hit the ball and the parents of that player saw everything that day, yet no one said a word to me or my son. It took over four years and several painful legal discoveries before the truth finally came out and a final settlement was reached. While I accepted that a teenager could make a mistake of that magnitude, it took me much longer to accept that adults could too.

After the injury, I was sidelined for a long time because I lost some of my speech and hearing abilities. Consequently I had to work with a speech pathologist for nearly nine months to try and get back on track. One of my strategies was to write everything down because I had speech aphasia—word-finding issues. Aphasia can occur after a stroke or a head injury. It is a condition that can rob you of your ability to communicate effectively.[3] In my case, I knew what I wanted to say, I just could not always find the words, or the correct words in the proper sequence to communicate what I wanted or needed to say. This meant sometimes I would speak in incomplete sentences—if I was under stress it seemed to make these symptoms worsen.

Moreover, like Dory in *Finding Nemo*, I was left with STM: short-term memory loss. This meant I could not return to the work I loved: facilitating focus groups for high-end corporate executives. I quickly realized that vice-presidents do not like to wear nametags, and people were not going to pay me thousands of dollars a day to ask them to repeat themselves because I could not follow their conversations. As one friend described me after my injury: "You're still you, Jane, but sometimes you're just delightfully ditzy." Whether I liked it or not, I had to accept this new reality in my life and that it was time for a change.

That's when I discovered there are two kinds of change: planned and unplanned.

Planned change is a conscious choice or decision. This might include changing your career, buying a house, getting married, or deciding to cut out the loaded fries and load up on protein shakes.

Unplanned change is an unexpected event or consequence of a circumstance. This may include a job loss, illness, divorce, a pandemic, or all of the above. Consequently, Clayton and

---

3. Mayoclinic.org/aphasia

I had already, in a very short period of time together, experienced a lot of unplanned change.

Clayton gazed at me intently from his hospital bed. "How did we meet?"

Over the years, my company had collaborated with Clayton and his firm very successfully on many complex, detailed projects. It had all started when I needed a disability study for a not-for-profit on a tight budget. Clayton was the CEO of the only market-research firm who offered to discount the work. This spoke volumes to me about his integrity and character.

After that project, Clayton invited me to come on board and help run his firm, but I declined. I had a successful company of my own, and I enjoyed my independence. However, I did tell him I would be happy to work together on projects with him from time to time. Henceforth, whenever he needed help to negotiate a tough business deal, he called me in for back up. My unofficial title was Vice-President in Charge of Conversation.

A few years later, Clayton walked into the office one day when I was there and said, "You look terrible."

I was going through a divorce, which was taking its toll. Simultaneously I was also parenting two active teenage boys and managing a flourishing career. Clayton offered to take me to dinner, and I accepted.

I was expecting to talk business, but he shocked me during the main course when he looked at me and said, "Jane, I could walk around the world a million times and never find another woman like you. If you ever want to date, I'd like to be first in line."

Needless to say, he had me at hello.

And now, sitting at the edge of his bed in the ICU step-down unit, looking into those kind, confused, twinkly-blue eyes, I realized that if Clayton was ever going to have a fighting chance at recovery on any level, he was going to need an advocate. Like it or not, to do this, I was going to have to accept more change and more responsibility. Instead of being Vice President in Charge of Conversation, I was going to have to be the CEO now—of everything.

> Acceptance is the first step towards successfully navigating change of any kind, especially rapid unplanned change.
> To move forward, not backward, one has to try and accept change has occurred, not resist or deny it.

Dear friends and family,

A super stressful day for C and me, kind of like being on one of those big, dangerous rollercoasters at an amusement park. By the way, I hate those rides, and although I never asked him, I am pretty sure C does too.

It all started when I woke up to an alert on my iPhone and news from my family of a tsunami warning for Vancouver Island. It was triggered by a massive quake of 8.2 off the coast of Alaska. Similar to the earthquake, C's blood pressure peaked at 240 over something last night. The nurses moved him twice as he kept getting out of bed to "go to the office" because he had an 8.2 quake in his head. The resident had transferred him to the neurosurgical ward after I left for the evening. After many telephone calls back and forth, the resident finally caved and transferred C back to the ICU, where he should have stayed in the first place.

Until today, I did not know it was humanly possible to have your blood pressure rise this high. It's super serious and very painful for your brain, especially with a fractured skull.

Blissfully, C cannot remember a thing about the previous night. Wouldn't we all like this to happen once in a while? Kind of like that movie The Hangover, *but with no tiger in the bathroom. All kidding aside, C is in a lot of pain. It is tough for him and tough for me to watch.*

So today we went for an emergency CT scan; even Sagoo, C's doctor, was worried. I love Dr. Sagoo for his skill and expertise, but dislike him because he doesn't listen to common sense. Sagoo avoided me all morning during rounds because he knew I was going to blast him. He also marked the CT urgent and ordered the porter and a nurse to wait while they did the scan so C could be closely monitored.

Outcome: no further bleeding, but still lots of pressure and swelling in C's head. Blood pressure more stable but not great, and thankfully Sagoo and I are still speaking.

On a positive note, I had lovely calls from two rabbis who are very concerned about C. He has two rabbis praying for him, plus so many treasured friends and my family, which is all wonderful. I am so thankful for this, and C would be too if he knew what was happening to him. Let's hope tomorrow will be more positive than today was.

Love to all . . . Jane

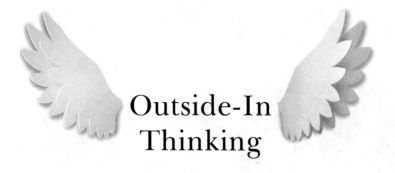

Outside-In
Thinking

CHAPTER THREE

Going to the Office

....

"Nobody likes a change except a wet baby."
—PETER DRUCKER

Welcome to Day 12, I think.

I say, "I think," because unless I look at the dates on my emails, I truly am not able to tell you how many days we have been here. I call this "hamster-wheel syndrome". I can only hope Merriam Webster or Wikipedia coins this phrase, as I am certain I'm not the first person to feel this way while supporting a loved one in the hospital.

For the past few nights, Clayton has been in CEO mode again. Late last night, while he was "going to the office", he pulled out his PICC line. A PICC line is a special IV line that patients can have inserted so they don't have to get poked with needles quite so often. It is special order and not easy to get.

This is just one of the laundry list of items that I negotiated with Dr. Sagoo to help ease discomfort for Clayton. However, Clayton probably thought he might get to the office a little faster with one less tube in him, so he decided to pull

17

it out. Anyway, he bought himself another day in the quiet, well-monitored ICU, as Sagoo deemed him a flight risk. Every cloud has a silver lining.

Clayton was still in CEO mode this morning when I arrived. He greeted me, his catheter bag in hand, and announced that the hospital was "way off" on all their measurements (blood pressure, inputs, outputs, etc.). Consequently, he was going to have to "monitor things more closely." I gently informed him that all was well—that, effective 12:01 a.m. EST, I had promoted myself from Vice President in Charge of Conversation to CEO of Everything, and I was monitoring the situation closely too.

In business, there is a lot of emphasis on monitoring things closely, especially when it comes to change. However people don't always take the same approach to change in their personal lives.

Business owners, corporate leaders, and executives spend billions of dollars discussing organizational change: how to define their mission and vision; and prepare, plan, respond to, and monitor their ever-changing markets and environments. Successful business leaders understand that in order to help your business thrive, make your company profitable, and keep your shareholders happy, you need to be mindful of what is happening now. You need to be flexible, adaptable, and receptive to change. You need to be able to envision the outcomes you desire and take the steps necessary to make your ideas happen. They understand that if you were to sell your product or service the same way for weeks, months, or years, without any consideration for your changing environment, or your customer's needs, you would fall behind the curve and be out of business—fast. In other words, successful business leaders embrace change and see the benefits and necessity of doing so.

On the flip side, when it comes to our personal lives, many individuals are resistant to change. How often have you heard someone say, "I hate change"? That's because most people do. In 1994, I had the pleasure and privilege to meet Peter Drucker, a respected expert in organizational change management. When I asked him for one piece of advice about life, he said, "Jane, nobody likes a change except a wet baby."

Fear of the unknown can be a big barrier to change. Most people are resistant to change because change takes us out of our comfort zones—that place, good or bad, where we know things are predictable. That's why often people stay in situations that perhaps they shouldn't such as a relationship or a job that isn't as fulfilling or healthy as it could be. The comfort of predictability can be just as strong as fear of the unknown, especially when unplanned change is contemplated or happens.

With no end in sight to this merry-go-round, my intuition told me that being resistant to change in this situation was not going to help anyone. Good or bad, I needed to embrace more change, not fear it. I decided my first order of business as CEO of Everything was to get my ducks in a row. Or in business-speak, complete an environmental scan to find clarity of thought.

An environmental scan is essentially a review of the strengths, weaknesses, opportunities, and threats for a given scenario. It is a staple in the business world when developing a strategic plan. Prior to my concussion, I probably completed over 500 scans for clients. They paid me to do this because most people are unable to see their companies—or their lives—with the clarity that comes from being on the outside looking in, rather than on the inside looking out. While Clayton was monitoring things closely on the night shift with the nurses, I found a pen. On the back of his hospital menu, I started to make notes looking at the situation from an outside in perspective.

Under strengths, I noted that Clayton had a strong will to live, a curious mind, and a high IQ, and that at this juncture his social skills were still relatively intact. He also had me as his advocate. Looking around this hospital unit, it was clear to me that a lot of patients didn't have that.

With regard to challenges, it was obvious his memory was a still a train wreck. Over the past few days, I'd asked four different neurosurgeons the following question: "On a scale of one to seven, with one being not serious at all and seven being the most serious ever, how serious is this latest traumatic brain injury (TBI) for Clayton?"

Independent of each other, they all gave it the same score. A five out of seven—numeric code for a life-altering brain injury. When pressed for answers, Dr. Sagoo told me candidly that he was not worried about Clayton's ability to recover physically, or about him losing any IQ points or his intellect. However, between the first bike accident, the car accident, and the subsequent fall in the garage, Clayton had a lot of trauma inside his brain, including frontal lobe damage.

Your frontal lobe is essentially your brain manager. The frontal lobe regulates working and secondary memory, impulse control, behaviour, problem solving, and judgement.[4] Essentially, it is the part of your brain that is responsible for the ability to decide between good and bad choices.[5] In other words, with this type of injury, it is very usual for the common-sense switch inside your frontal lobe to get turned off, either intermittingly or all together. I also learned from Dr. Sagoo that when a person has had a previous TBI, the likelihood of them experiencing a subsequent TBI and reinjuring themselves increases dramatically.[6] Therefore, Dr. Sagoo was adamant that keeping Clayton out of harm's way during and

---

4. Wikipedia.org/frontallobeinjury

5. Ibid

6. National Brain Association of Canada: nbia.ca/statistics

after his recovery was essential. He could not hit his head again, even a teeny-weeny bit. The next time, it could be fatal.

On the opportunities side, Clayton's will to live and get better was going to be essential to move forward with anything. His high IQ and laundry list of accomplishments were assets, but also threats. Finding new ways to stimulate his keen mind on a daily basis and keep him out of trouble might be a problem in the future.

After I got my ducks in a row bedside with a SWOT, I found the clarity of thought I was looking for. I realized that all of my business experience to date had prepared me for this event. I already had the skills I needed to help both Clayton and me navigate this situation; I just needed to apply them in a different context.

I decided on Day 12 that the only way for both of us to come out the other end of this experience successfully was to look at this unplanned change from the outside in, rather than the inside out. I needed to treat this life-altering event as a project: Project Memory.

Fear of the unknown can be a barrier to change.

An environmental scan is a tool we can use to help us look at change more objectively—from the outside-in, rather than the inside-out.

Looking at your scenario from the outside-in can help you more readily accept change, reduce fear, and see the big picture.

....

Dear friends and family,

Project Memory: I Have An Idea: Can You Help, Please?

Today I showed C a get-well card he had received. He was like a kid opening a present. He loved opening the envelope and was very touched that someone would take time to think of him. I believe it would really help lift his spirits and help his memory if friends could continue to send him a card, or an email, along with a picture of yourself, with your good wishes. Maybe take a selfie?

To help put the importance of this project into context:

When you've hit your head and have a TBI, it's like a filing cabinet has fallen over and the contents have spilled on the floor. Sometimes, all the files do not get put back in the right place. That is what has happened to C. He needs help to remember things and put all the cards back in the filing cabinet in the right order.

C can still talk about politics and world events very well. However, he cannot remember what happened a day ago, or the day before that. Intellectually, he knows things are different, but his judgement and memory are compromised.

Connecting a face with your good wishes will hopefully help him put people into context and focus on the positives. It will also remind him he is well thought of. Keeping a positive attitude will expedite and assist in his recovery enormously.

So, be thankful for your memory and your good health, and please keep those cards, calls, and emails coming. We both sincerely appreciate and need them—especially on Day 12.
Love to all and I look forward to receiving your emails and cards for him.
Till next time . . . Jane

....

CHAPTER FOUR

Going to the
Principal's Office

···

*"It's not about the cards you're dealt,
but how you play the hand."*
—RANDY PAUSCH

I decided to put on my interior decorating hat and was working with Clayton bedside to try and brighten up his hospital room. We were pasting cards and pictures people had sent for Project Memory onto bright-yellow Bristol board. I had taken a cue from my stint as a kindergarten teacher years ago in a remote First Nation community near Hudson's Bay. The town I taught in had fewer than 500 people, and the only way to get there was to fly in by small plane. Resources like paper and art supplies were hard to come by, so you had to be very creative. To brighten things up, I had taken pictures of the children with a Polaroid camera and displayed photographs beside their work to decorate the classroom.

I held up a photo for Clayton. "This is David and Anna; we went on vacation with them last year to France."

Since Clayton still wasn't able to remember faces, he needed help to sift through the cards and pictures to match the correct person to their card and identify the context of his relationship to them. So, on Day 15 we got our Martha Stewart on and started tacking up cards and pictures so he could match the person to their name—my version of Hospital Pictionary.

"Ms. Enright, have you got a minute?" Leila, the occupational therapist, was calling to me from the doorway. She motioned me over to the nurses' station. "Clayton seems to be doing better; it's so nice to see him more relaxed."

After many "gentle reminders," the healthcare team *finally* seemed to be accepting my suggestions of regular, low-dose pain relief rather than relying on Clayton to tell them when, and if, he had pain. Remember, this was the guy with no short-term memory. Quite frankly, this suggestion seemed like a no-brainer to me.

"I wanted to chat with you for a moment, Ms. Enright, and share Clayton's MoCA test score."

The MoCA test is short for the Montreal Cognitive Assessment. The Montreal Cognitive Assessment is a brief, thirty-question screening tool that is widely used as an assessment for detecting cognitive impairment. It was developed by a group at McGill University. A score of 26 or over is considered normal. People without cognitive impairment score an average of 27.4. People with mild cognitive impairment (MCI), score an average of 22.1; people with Alzheimer's disease score an average of 16.2.[7]

"How did he do?"

She pulled out a piece of paper from her clipboard and pointed to his score. I quickly did the math, which was not

---

7. Wikipedia.org/Montreal Cognitive Assessment

easy because I hate math. In fact, I failed Grade 9 math, twice. However, it didn't take a math wizard to interpret this score.

I looked back at Clayton, who was staring at his cards. There is a saying that life is not about the cards you're dealt, it's how you play them. My approach to life had always been positive. I treat others as I would want to be treated. I am a kind person, and so is Clayton. We work hard, help our family, friends, and neighbours, and try our best. Looking at Clayton on Day 15, I could not help but think we had both been dealt a very bad hand.

Between my head injury, Clayton's first concussion, and this latest turn of events, I felt like a schoolgirl who was being punished for something. It seemed as if I was being sent to the principal's office over and over and over again, except I didn't know what I was being reprimanded for. I was pondering a lot of explanations for these events—everything from: Maybe I was a really bad person in another life, to, what did I do to deserve this, to these events must be happening for a reason. I found myself digging deep for answers to spiritual questions that were haunting me.

Theories abound about religion and spirituality. According to experts they do overlap, however people often confuse the two.[8] Religion is a set of organized beliefs usually shared by a community or group with faith-based boundaries. Religion typically questions what is right or wrong. Spirituality is a broader concept with room for many perspectives. In general, spirituality includes a sense of connection to something bigger than ourselves, and typically involves a search for meaning such as where do I personally find connection and value in life.[9]

---

8. University of Minnesota: Taking Charge of Your Health & Well Being: takingcharge.csh.umn.edu/What is Spirituality
9. Ibid

When bad things happen, as we try to find answers and meaning, it is very common to internalize our emotions and feelings. Our thoughts are powerful, and people often become a reflection of their thought patterns. Because fear is a barrier to change, when we view situations we can make decisions or come to conclusions that are fear-based, rather than faith-based; we emphasize and focus on the negative, rather than on the positive. In the process we can sometimes be quick to judge ourselves, or others, harshly. As we navigate change and decision-making, quite often we forget to introduce an element of humour to mitigate this. During times of unexpected change, it requires diligence to focus our thoughts on the positive and to pay attention to these positive thoughts. If we don't, our own thoughts can get in our own way and we can get caught in the weeds when it comes to decision-making.

I handed Leila back the MoCA test sheet. "Can he have a re-do?"

Leila looked at me in earnest, and then said matter-of-factly, "I'm sorry, but we cannot repeat tests. We already did a baseline before this one. This is his second test, and we are not allowed to do more than that."

"So, what does that mean?"

"It means we are a neurosurgical unit and unfortunately not equipped to handle someone who is at risk of re-injury. Carolyn, the physiotherapist and I looked at the pictures you brought in of your residence. The layout—it's all stairs. Clayton cannot fall and injure himself again. In our opinion, with his balance and memory issues, he needs more care than this hospital ward or you, can provide."

After my conversations with Sagoo and the neurosurgical team, I was not surprised to hear this statement. I was, however, still coming to terms with this reality. "What about the Acquired Brain Injury (ABI) program?"

The ABI program is a community re-integration program that supports individuals with moderate-to-severe brain injuries. Treatment focuses on regaining a level of independence in order to reintegrate into the community.[10] A very nice resident from the ABI program had visited Clayton while he was still in the ICU step-down unit. Unfortunately, because of his memory issues, Clayton had not passed the test she administered for entry into the program.

"They have a long wait list, Ms. Enright. Due to the severity of his injuries and his age, you need to start looking at options that will keep him out of harm's way—he cannot stay here." Leila's pager went off. "I'm sorry, I have to go to another floor." She handed me a sheet of paper. "Please let me know your choices by the end of this week, so we can get the paperwork started."

After Leila left, I looked at the sheet she'd handed me. Her options consisted of long-term care facilities and some therapeutic day programs. I knew Clayton better than anyone else. If he went into a nursing home now, that would be the last stop for him. Instead of progressing, he would go backwards. Even with all this trauma, he still had a big brain, and he needed to use it. Right now, it seemed like he was stuck in the principal's office too. He didn't meet the criteria to remain where he was, yet he was being told he was not well enough for a program to help him get better. He wanted to return home, but if he did, he was at risk of seriously reinjuring himself.

I searched for the rehab resident's business card and pulled out my cell phone. Although I didn't know it yet, outside-in thinking was helping me to move forward while I sorted out why we both seemed to be going to the principal's office all the time.

---

10. hamiltonhealthsciences.ca/ABI

When bad things happen, it is very common to internalize our feelings.

Looking outside-in reduces emotionality, so we can find clarity of thought and uncover answers when we need them.

Outside-in thinking helps us not get caught in the weeds as we navigate change.

....

Dear friends and family,

You know you have been in the hospital too long when . . .

> *. . . you are there for shift change, and you know 6/7 of the night nurses by their first names*
> *. . . the parking lot attendant, who looks like a motorcycle gang member but is extremely polite and decent (we can't judge a book by its cover), offers to "save you a spot" for the next day*
> *. . . 6/7 nurses know YOU by your first name*
> *. . . you start exchanging recipes with the cleaning staff*
> *. . . the coffee lady offers you a discount*
> *. . . you return to the parking lot the next day to claim your "reserved space", someone tries to take it, and biker guy tells the other driver to get the f—out of your spot*

True stories . . .

Because C has relatively no short-term memory or retention, every day, several times a day, he asks me how long he has been "here." He has been "here" fifteen days or 360 hours . . . that's an hour for each day in a year. This can make one begin to contemplate how one is spending one's time.

C had his second shower today in fifteen days. We take these things for granted, like being able to step into the shower unassisted. He still needs lots of help but looks and feels a lot better. He is slowly but surely making progress, and I am working with the team here to determine next steps.

BTW: Please keep the cards and pictures coming! I put on my interior decorating hat and hung up your cards on the wall along with the pictures you sent—C loved it. The nurses read them to him, too, to help remind him he is well thought of. It perks him up.

Finally, a big thanks to my friend Jenn and my Fundas friends who are keeping us well fed. Jenn set up a wonderful website to coordinate meal preparation and delivery from everyone. Please know we are all so grateful to all of you. Especially Ross, who is at university and comes home for care packages, and Ryan, who is at home waiting for me for dinner; the boys haven't eaten this well since they visited their grandparents!

Love to all and thanks for your continued support.
Best,
Jane

....

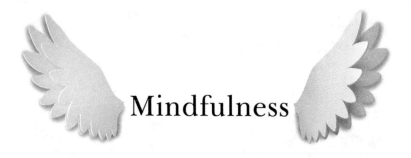

Mindfulness

CHAPTER FIVE

One Day at a Time

....

"Don't count the days,
make the days count."

—MUHAMMAD ALI

When I arrived on the neurosurgical unit at lunchtime, Clayton was nowhere to be found. Yes, I know what you are thinking. . . . Thankfully, he had just taken a stroll down the hall with his physiotherapist and his walker. I found him in the sunroom, sitting in earnest conversation, chatting up some ladies. From what I could see, he had quite a captive audience too. When I asked if he wanted to join me for lunch, he said, "Well, yes," but he preferred to stay awhile longer so he could get to know his new friends.

"What's that?" Clayton was glancing up at the television screen in the sunroom.

Clayton was like Curious George now. He asked questions about everything—sometimes the same one over and over again. He could not control this; it was his brain trying to learn how to process information again.

"That's skiing."

"What's skiing?"

Clayton remembered who I was now, but he did not remember I had visited him the day before, or the day before that—he seemed to have no sense of time. He still did not remember the house we shared, his address, what city he lived in, or that the building he was staying in was called a hospital. He also didn't seem to remember that in his early twenties, he had skied in the French Alps a few times.

On the upside, he did have snippets of memory about past events from time to time. With prompting, Clayton remembered that he had been invited to Washington to attend the inauguration of his friend, a retired admiral who was being appointed as the US ambassador to Norway. He also kept asking me why it was a cloudy day today. I had to explain to him that it was cloudy because it was wintertime, and remind him that it was February and that in winter we do not have as much sun as we do in the spring or the summer. This may seem bizarre, because at first glance, it is.

Yet, sitting in that sunroom, looking at things from the outside in, instead of the inside out, I slowly began to realize what no health professional, or MoCA test, had been able to explain for the past eighteen days. I began to understand that at that moment, because Clayton could neither remember the past nor focus on the future, his mind was in a constant state of present. However, in Clayton's case, his mindfulness appeared to be on steroids.

The University of California, Berkeley, defines mindfulness as: "The practice of maintaining a nonjudgmental state of heightened awareness of one's thoughts, emotions, or experiences on a moment-to-moment basis."[11]

My translation: *Mindfulness is like one, big, continuous AA meeting. You take each day, one day at a time.*

---

11. Greater Good Science Centre, University of California, Berkeley, https://greatergood.berkeley.edu/mindfulness

There is a lot of emphasis on mindfulness these days—people also spend a great deal of money trying to achieve it. They buy books, go to classes, listen to podcasts, practice yoga, meditate, and explore wellness retreats to try to stay in the present moment during everyday life. There are many benefits to being mindful such as improving our emotional and physical well-being.[12] What many people don't realize is that mindfulness is not just an everyday tool; it can also be a strategy we call upon to support us to successfully navigate change. This is because staying present can help us reduce distress about the past and worry about the future.

Nonetheless, when unexpected change happens, it can be extremely difficult to remain mindful—especially if you happen to be the CEO of Everything. Let's face it; you have a lot on your mind. This can include thoughts about what might have been (depression) and/or thoughts about what might or might not happen next (anxiety about the future). During the day, I was putting on my cheery cheerleader routine at the hospital, but at night, on my own while I tossed and turned, it was another story. I was anxious about what was going to happen next.

For Clayton, it was the complete opposite. Because he could not remember the past nor anticipate the future, he was neither depressed nor anxious. At this moment he was just present. Clayton was not counting the days, because it was impossible for him to do so. He was making the days count. As I watched Clayton in the sunroom, I suddenly realized that along with all of this trauma he had been given a wonderful gift; a gift many people work hard to achieve daily. He was a walking, talking infomercial for mindfulness. At that moment, if I could have bottled his brain, we would have both been millionaires.

My cell phone rang. "Hello?"

---

12. Harvard Health Publishing, Harvard Medical School Help Guide: helpguide.org /benefitsofmindfulness

"Hi Ms. Enright, it's Dr. Neshima returning your call from the rehabilitation centre."

Dr. Neshima was the nice resident who had visited Clayton in the ICU step-down unit. I had telephoned her to see if she could return to assess Clayton for admission to the Acquired Brain Injury Program (ABI). Not just anybody gets into the ABI rehab program. It is a one-of-a-kind program that caters to people like Clayton who have had brain injuries via traumatic events. Beds are in short supply, and people from across Canada are on a wait list.

"Thanks for returning my call," I said. "I was reaching out to you about my partner. You visited him about a week ago to see if he was a candidate for ABI."

"Ahh yes, I remember."

"He is on the neurosurgical ward now. You indicated he could be reassessed after he left the ICU. I was hoping you could come back and re-evaluate him."

"I'm sorry, but as it happens, my residency rotation is finishing tomorrow. I'm leaving to go to another hospital."

My stomach lurched. I knew in my heart that if Clayton was not accepted into the ABI program, he would be done and dusted. "Can someone else evaluate him?"

She paused and then said, "That might be challenging. Just wait one moment; I'll check."

I waited for what seemed like an eternity. I tried to take a cue from Clayton and be mindful, but my anxiety level was rising exponentially by the minute.

At last she returned. "My colleague Matt is beginning his rotation today. I can schedule him for the day after tomorrow."

I jumped up and down in the sunroom. Maybe, just maybe, we were finally going to get out of the principal's office! I covered my cellphone: "C, great news! I think we might get a hall pass!"

Clayton gave me the biggest smile ever.

"That's great J. What's a hall pass?"

38

Being mindful can help us reduce sadness about the past and anxiety about the future.

Mindfulness is a tool that can help support us to stay positive as we navigate change.

....

Dear friends and family,

C explained to me once that in the Jewish faith the number eighteen stands for life, and anything divisible by eighteen is a lucky number. Not being Jewish, I am sure his rabbi could provide a much more fulsome explanation than I have, but you get the gist of it.

Today is the eighteenth day that C has been in the hospital, and today may be the tipping point to get him that bed in rehab. His physician came by this afternoon and told us flat out, "Your rehabilitation assessment is in forty-eight hours, and I need your bed."

He then proceeded to coach C about passing the test—not kidding. The doctor told C to get to bed early and that he must look alert and motivated. Given that healthcare is often a numbers game of supply and demand, the doctor is doing the arithmetic and everything in between to ensure C gets a spot, so he can open up another one.

C told me very seriously today that he wants to live another fifty years. He is still very articulate and alert but, understandably, gets jumbled sometimes. We did the math together, and I told him while living another fifty years might be a bit of "an aggressive schedule," he had the right mindset. He wants to live, move forward, and get better.

Thank goodness C is being considered for rehab—a lot of people leave the hospital without the support they need and may not make it. On that note, please pray to the rehab fairies for us!

Love to all . . . Jane

CHAPTER SIX

Life Is Not a Textbook

···

*"Not everything that counts can be counted, and
not everything that can be counted counts."*

—ALBERT EINSTEIN

M att, the resident, arrived with his textbook at 10:30 a.m. to assess Clayton. He looked like the Doogie Howser of rehab—about sixteen years old.

Despite his injuries Clayton picked up on this right away, and in typical Clayton fashion said, "Young man, I have been a professor for forty years, and you look very intelligent, but, quite honestly, you don't look older than twenty. How old are you?"

Matt, (aka the kid), took it with a grain of salt and said to Clayton, "We'll come back to that later."

Even with this injury, Clayton is still very intelligent and a critical thinker. However, the location of the bleeding had affected his speech, memory, and cognition. He could hold a conversation with you, but ironically, like me after my head injury, he had trouble finding his words.

The kid asked Clayton a battery of questions, including what he knew about survey research.

Clayton replied, "I'm sorry, young man, but I don't know a thing about it."

Clayton still had vivid memories of being a professor, but had few memories about his company or being a CEO. He remembered who the prime minister was and some government policy, but just then he could not tell you if he had brushed his teeth, eaten his breakfast, or what day of the week it was. At that moment, he couldn't remember where he lived one day to the next, or activities throughout the day. He might or might not have remembered your face or your name. He might know he knew you, but not be able to say your name. Matt quickly determined that as of today, Clayton's short-term recall and retention were still moderately compromised.

After looking at his textbook, the kid also quickly determined that on top of all his other conditions, Clayton had PTA: post-traumatic amnesia. PTA is the brain's way of coping with stress. It blocks out a memory of a traumatic event and usually anything remotely related to it.[13] This can sometimes last a lifetime and memories may or may not return. This explains why, weeks after the accident, Clayton could not remember our home or who I was. Similar to my head injury, the kid equated Clayton's condition to that of Dory's in *Finding Nemo*—short-term memory (STM) issues, but on a grander scale.

This made perfect sense and explained a lot. I had to give Matt credit because Sagoo, the neurosurgeon with fourteen years of education, had not picked up on this. The bad news was that because Clayton could not retain information, he was, according to the kid and his textbook, "Not a good candidate for rehab at this time."

---

13. December 13, 2017, medicalnewstoday.com/What_is_amnesia_and_how_is_it_treated

This was because Clayton could learn, but would not necessarily retain what he had learned. Nonetheless, while Clayton was answering questions incorrectly, he was providing answers in such a way that the kid realized how intelligent he was. Matt was, in a word, "awestruck" by Clayton's ability to circumvent the question. He called Clayton crafty—I called him strategic. Even so, the kid said, based on Clayton's score and his textbook, he did not think Clayton could get into the ABI program.

I could tell right away Matt was intuitive. Nonetheless, he did not understand yet that many of the things you can count in life, don't count, and many of the things you can't count, really count. For instance, a textbook could not measure that Clayton was a proven performer with a solid track record of accomplishments. Nor could it measure Clayton's zest and enthusiasm for life, or sheer determination and will to live after a catastrophic injury. A textbook could not capture that Clayton was a lifelong learner with a positive attitude who wanted to continue to learn, and recover. Moreover, a textbook did not grasp that if the kid didn't take a flyer on him, Clayton's outcomes would be grim. What the kid also clearly did not understand was that I was the CEO of Everything now, and tired of going to the principal's office with Clayton all the time.

There is a quote by Hugh Prather that says: "There is a time to let things happen and there is a time to make things happen." And so I replied, "You strike me as bright, Matt. Bright enough to know that each individual's journey is unique; that life is not a textbook. Here are five reasons why you should let him in."

I gave the presentation of my life.

After my spiel he replied, "I need to go talk to my boss."

Each individual's journey is unique.

Accepting that your journey is unique helps you stay mindful and removes the temptation to judge yourself, and others, as you navigate change.

....

Dear friends and family,

I received a few worried texts and emails today from people inquiring if everything was still okay. First, I am so sorry I did not send an update yesterday; I did not intend to make anyone nervous. I just had an exceedingly busy day with the usual hospital stuff plus trying to get C into rehab.

At this point, we are still waiting to see if C will be admitted to the ABI program. To say we are in a holding pattern would be the understatement of the year.

To use some analogies, we are:

sitting in the green room waiting to go live on the Johnny Carson Show.

whales at MarineLand swimming in a tank that is way too small.

trying to tread water for four solid minutes to pass our swimming test at the YMCA, so we can go off the high board in the deep end.

It seems like C is slowly getting ready for his next step in recovery. However, he is also very frustrated, confused, and puzzled as to why he can't just walk out the door. He desperately wants to leave the hospital, but I told him he has to relearn some things first, like how to walk up and down stairs and talk to strangers safely. I equated rehab with going back to graduate school; every day he can consult the experts about his brain and learn new things.

Changing topics: R and R are heading west!

Some of you may not know that my sons have been planning a travel and work odyssey to Western Canada, Australia, and beyond after their graduation from university and secondary school.

Well, they made it happen! I am very proud to report that they have secured super-awesome jobs! After graduation, they both are going to be working at a world-class golf course in Alberta. From there, if things go well, they will continue to work and travel around the world.

This is such an exciting, wonderful moment in the middle of such a traumatic, difficult time. I will miss them terribly when they leave, but I am so very proud they were able to make this happen for themselves that I had to share it.

Love to all and thanks for hanging in there with us.

Jane

CHAPTER SEVEN

Just Like Amy Winehouse . . .

"Don't judge each day by the harvest you reap,
but by the seeds you plant."
—ROBERT LOUIS STEVENSON

The kid came through—big time. On Wednesday at 10:00 a.m., Clayton was transferred to the ABI program.

If I had to summarize Clayton's first week in rehab, I would say it was like a fast-paced game of dodge ball with lots of dips and dives.

When I asked him what he thought of rehab, Clayton was more succinct; he called it, "An undemocratic organization."

Clayton was used to calling the shots and being the boss, and he was very independent. This is a hard role to play in rehab because rehab is not a loosey-goosey, come-and-go-as-you-please kind of place. Rehab is all about safety first. The floor is monitored 24/7 because patients are an "elopement risk"; not because they want to run off and get married, but because everyone there has suffered a serious brain injury that leaves them vulnerable to compromised thinking, and risk of re-injury. Consequently, 3 South, where the ABI program is housed, is a locked ward.

Everyone in the ABI program was unique. Some patients were less ambulatory, and some, like Clayton, had more of an invisible disability. You also don't stay for a day or two in the ABI program and then leave; it is a process. It often takes months, sometimes years for brain injuries to heal. Patients are closely monitored and kept in a bit of a bubble for weeks and months, so they don't reinjure themselves. Activities are reintroduced slowly and carefully with a mind to preventing further injury or harm and promoting recovery.

For reasons that were still unknown, Clayton still could not seem to grasp the seriousness of his accident or its consequences. Because of this, from his perspective, he did not fit in. Understandably, he felt like he had stepped onto the wrong set of a Hollywood movie—and so did I. Instead of being *The Godfather*, he felt he had been miscast as a prisoner in *Escape from Alcatraz*. To make matters worse, as his brain was changing and recovering, his mindfulness was waning. Instead of making every day count, he was back to counting the days. Unfortunately Clayton also could not remember what he had just told you, so he tended to repeat himself—he couldn't help it.

Consequently, Clayton spent the whole week telling me the staff were incompetent, that he did not know why he was there, and that he saw no value to being in rehab. In his opinion, all he required were a few days in the program and some tips and tricks from the staff to cope with his injuries. After that, he would be on his way, and all would be well and good—thank you very much. This mantra happened every day from Monday to Sunday for approximately 112 hours—the staff can back me up on this.

After hours and days of "get me out of here" talk, I put on my CEO of Everything hat, called a board meeting, and gave Clayton my "Life Does Not Have To Be Difficult" lecture. From the title, you may think this is an "oh, poor you" kind of speech. In fact, it is quite the opposite. The My Life Does Not Have To Be Difficult lecture is premised on the reality that life is not fair, because it isn't. However, it's not about the cards you are dealt, or what other people do or do not do with their hands; it is how you play yours. That when you accept change, rather than try to push it away, your approach to life shifts dramatically, as do your outcomes.

I did not use my nice, patient, bright, cheerleader voice when I delivered this lecture; I also didn't pull any punches. I told Clayton that he had failed the test and almost did not get into the program, and that it was difficult to get him a spot. I emphasized that if he continued to criticize the staff, he would be the last one on their list to help. Moreover, he would be expelled from the program and would not get a second chance. I reminded him that he should be grateful he could still walk and talk, get around, breathe without a tube, and feed himself. I told him that I had faith he could do this and that he owed it to himself and me to give this program a chance and see where this could go. Then I gave him a hug, told him I believed in him, and left the hospital.

I wasn't proud that I lost my temper, or that I left. I was trying to be mindful, but I was exhausted and frustrated. Outside-in thinking was helping me understand that Clayton's memory was returning, but because of his injuries, he could not grasp or accept that he required ongoing intervention and assistance. Nonetheless, I was afraid that after all of this effort to get him into the program, any opportunity for recovery or improvements would be thrown away. After conversations with the staff, I could tell they were concerned too. We seemed to be going backwards, instead of forwards.

After my speech I got in my car and cried all the way home. When I got there, I realized that I couldn't carry this burden on my own anymore. That's when I sat down, poured myself a stiff drink, and prayed for a miracle.

Faith is believing in miracles when logic tells you that you should not.

Having faith that everything will work out helps you find strength and stay mindful as you transition through change.

....

Dear friends and family,

As we conclude week-one of rehab, C is less than thrilled about still being in the hospital. I have been putting on my super-patient and pleasant marketing hat, but I must admit C is one of my tougher clients and I am feeling stretched.

For example, after his first day in rehab, he greeted me with: "Jane, no one here knows what they are doing."

I indicated that while I appreciated this observation, if he was doing a survey, his sample would not meet Canadian market-research standards; he had only interviewed five respondents instead of the required one hundred. Moreover, he had only been present on the rehab unit for 6.5 hours. In other words, please try and give this a chance.

Given this current state of affairs, I am reaching out to share some ideas about how you can help C, and me, get through this rough patch:

1. *Sign up for a short visit. Weekends will be rough because programming is limited, and he can't leave the floor. Early evenings are good for visits*

too. Please email or call me if you want to visit this weekend.
2. *Send him a card or email with your favourite memory of him. We still welcome your cards and good wishes.*
3. *Please continue to keep connected with me.*

For those of you who don't know, I am juggling a lot right now. I had my own little setback last year when I was struck in the head with a volleyball at my son's tournament. I was sidelined from work, and activities, then this. Along with supporting C and my own recovery, I am trying to keep my business, and C's company, running—which is very challenging. Special thanks to my colleagues for assisting me while I try to stay afloat professionally.

Also, many of you have written or called to say you enjoy and appreciate my updates and "chatty" emails. My mother would tell you I was very talkative as a child—like a Chatty Cathy doll. I know, hard to believe. All kidding aside, your kind words warm my heart—many thanks for the kudos. Writing these updates is very therapeutic and helps keep me going. Likewise, a big shout-out to my FUNdas girlfriends Anna and Abigail who took me out to dinner and the movies this week, which was wonderfully normal. It is important for me to have a life too and connect with the outside world while we get through this.

Even though C is still adjusting to rehab, thankfully he is medically stable. Given that, I am going to move to weekly updates rather than daily updates. If something super-major happens, good or bad, I promise to update you.

Please know we sincerely appreciate all the good wishes, food, cards, support, and emails.
Love to all and thanks for hanging in there with us
. . . Jane

....

Gratitude

CHAPTER EIGHT

It's Not Really Rehab—
It's Tax Efficiency

....

"Life is lived forwards,
but understood backwards."
—SONIA KIERKEGAARD

The day after my lecture, I got a call from Clayton. I had been going to visit him in the morning, but he said he was tied up—he had a class to go to.

Since day one, I had been emphasizing to the staff the importance of Clayton connecting to and feeling vested with the ABI program. Because Clayton felt he did not belong, he did not feel there was much point in trying to fit in. If I were in his shoes, I would feel similarly too. However, he needed to make some new friends, to find someone to talk to and share meals with. I couldn't be with him 24/7. In my opinion, the staff wasn't paying enough attention to this, and consequently, it was making their job a hundred times more difficult. Given that, I was like Julie, the cruise director on

Love Boat. For days I scoured the ward with my imaginary clipboard looking for friend opportunities for Clayton. He had been refusing to participate in group activities, so this new development was encouraging.

It turned out the "class" was an outing to the Farmer's Market—a favourite destination. There he met Doug, an eighty-year-old armed forces veteran who had survived many conflicts and was now fighting his own battle; recovery from a brain injury he suffered when a saucepan fell off a shelf onto the top of his head. According to the occupational therapy staff Clayton was an absolute hit on the trip: charming, friendly, and extremely engaged. He also remembered going to the market before and was giving tips about the best vendors. When I arrived on Friday afternoon, Clayton was a different person. He greeted me with a smile and a beautiful bouquet of flowers he had chosen for me. He'd had a good day, and it only got better from there.

On Friday night, we stopped in the lounge to help Marnie. Marnie was a fifty-eight-year-old patient who'd had a brain aneurism and stroke as she was driving her car home from work. She had been bounced around between four hospitals over four months. Marnie had been admitted the same day as Clayton and guess what? Like Clayton she was bilingual! Marnie told him that out of all the hospitals she had been to, this was the best one; she had seen more progress in a week than in three months. As Marnie was relating her story, I could see Clayton's brain processing this insider information.

Clayton's mobility is much better than Marnie's, and Marnie's memory is better than Clayton's. That evening, Clayton helped Marnie change the TV channels and get her food out of the refrigerator. Marnie helped Clayton remember he had food in the refrigerator and that it was time to eat. We made a pact that I would bring Marnie food in from the other side, and Marnie promised she would look out for C.

I couldn't have been happier for him. He had found some friends and allies, plus I think Julie, the cruise director, would have been proud too.

Then, after several difficult days, we had another breakthrough. Clayton casually said to me, "Jane, I hope during this recovery period we are managing our affairs as tax efficiently as possible."

For two weeks I had been racking my brain to try and explain the value of rehab to Clayton in a way that would resonate with him. Similar to my Life Does Not Have To Be Difficult speech, I was trying to emphasize the concept of gratitude; that despite these challenges, there were so many things to be grateful for, such as receiving an abundance of healthcare from people who cared. Furthermore, due to Canada's universal health care system, Clayton was able to receive services without financial stress. Most importantly, despite a plethora of events, he was lucky to be alive. Until now, all of my attempts to help him be grateful had been unsuccessful.

Not any more—bingo, I now had the lingo I had been so desperately searching for! Of course I had been promoting gratitude all along; I just had not been using terminology that resonated with him. I then proceeded to brainstorm all the things we could be grateful for, including receiving services "in house" rather than as an out-patient that were thankfully provided by the universal health plan he had supported for years.

As we concluded Day 29, was everything rosy and perfect at the ABI Program? No way, not a chance. Tax efficiency planning is hard work. However, at least we seemed to be going forward instead of backwards—a breakthrough that I am very thankful for!

Moving backwards sometimes before we go forward is a normal part of adjusting to change.

When this happens, it is hard to stay positive.

Gratitude is a powerful tool that can help us get back on track and stay positive so we can successfully navigate change.

Dear friends and family,

While C remains "less than enthusiastic" about his stay in rehab, he has made solid progress. He is participating during activities, making some new friends, and in his words, is "feeling stronger each day."

To help cheer him up, last week I snuck my dog Buddy into the rehab unit. Buddy is a ninety-pound black Labrador retriever. Now, for those of you who know Buddy, you are probably saying to yourselves, "Oh my gosh, Jane, what were you thinking?"

Buddy is ten years going on ten months, and very enthusiastic. He also thinks he is a lap dog. I figured if Curious George could go to the hospital, why not Buddy? So, on one of those icy days early last week, I looked at Buddy and said, "Field trip," and I drove with him to the ABI Program.

For the record, Buddy hates riding in the car. He has actually jumped out the window to chase a squirrel—twice, when the car was still moving. Therefore, I avoid driving him anywhere like the plague. However, this time Buddy did not make a peep. I think somehow he knew this trip was an important one. When we got to 3 South, I sheepishly walked up to the nurse's station with

Buddy and said, "I'm so sorry, I know I am breaking the rules, but I just thought this might help C settle in."

The nurse looked at me and said with a wink, "Geez, ya gotta love these service dog programs! How nice of you to visit, especially on a Sunday. Please ensure you visit each and every patient."

Buddy was on his very best behaviour. He greeted all the patients affectionately and did not bark once. In fact, he was such a hit that Matt, the resident (aka "the kid"), asked me on the way out when the next visit was scheduled. When I laughed and said I did not want to jinx it, he said, "Don't worry, Ms. Enright . . . life is not a textbook."

Love to all, and thanks for hanging in there with us.
Jane

....

CHAPTER NINE

You Did It, My Friend— Congratulations on Your Thirty-Day Challenge!

....

"Beautiful souls are shaped by ugly experiences."

—MATSHONA DHLIWAYO

"Should I bring you the breakfast sandwich, or would you prefer the spinach wrap with egg and cheese?"

It was Saturday morning, and my best friend Jenn was calling me from the drive thru. It had been over a month since Clayton's accident, and I hadn't seen her for weeks. She was coming over to catch up before I headed back to the hospital.

"By the way, is this a boozy breakfast? Should I pick up bloody-mary mix too?

In September 1978, I won the lottery. I won the lottery because I had the pleasure, privilege, and good fortune of meeting my best friend of forty years, Jennifer Jean. Jenn is so joyful, and she brings so much joy to others. She has this lovely smile and a great big laugh that lights up a room. That laugh goes all the way from the top of her head to the tips of her toes: She radiates happiness when she laughs.

I first saw that great big laugh when we were twelve years old and Jenn invited me to stay for the weekend at her parents' chalet in Beaver Valley. It was Friday night, and everyone had gone to bed. It was pitch black in the house when I got up in the middle of the night to use the bathroom. I flipped on the light, and what's the first thing I see? A set of teeth in a glass on the shelf. It turns out those were her dad's teeth. I had never seen anything like this before. I screamed so loud that I woke up the whole house. Jenn came running, and when she saw how gobsmacked I was, she laughed so hard that her whole body shook. We all laughed, and this was the start of many happy times together with her family at Beaver Valley Ski Club.

At Beaver Valley, Jenn's dad taught me how to ski, and her mom taught me about après ski. We would get up early in the morning, pack our lunches, and Jenn's dad would drive us to the top of the run. Many days, Jenn and I were the last ones off the hill. Riding the chairlift and skiing those trails was where our friendship grew. It was at Beaver Valley that we bonded and became inseparable.

When we returned to the cottage at the end of the day, Jenn's mom would often be sitting on the deck watching the sunset in her raccoon-fur coat with a glass of wine. She taught us about Happy Hour and the importance of putting ice in your drink so you wouldn't get hungover. Of course, these are crucial life lessons. Most importantly, I learned from Jenn and her family how to have fun and seize the day. It was because of Jenn that I fell in love with skiing—an activity I thoroughly enjoy and share to this day with my children. I also fell in love with beautiful Beaver Valley.

"I'll have the spinach wrap, please. And by the way, perhaps you should add booze to all those dinner drop-offs too."

In the middle of all this chaos, not only was Jenn making and dropping off dinners for Clayton and my family, she had set up a webpage to organize our other friends so they could do so too. Delicious meals from my FUNdas girlfriends would appear on the porch—a welcome act of kindness during a tough time. At the heart of it, Jenn is a doer. She had done more in fifty-one years than most people might do in a hundred. She was always the first one to volunteer to organize things, so everyone could come together, get things done, and have a good time. When I called her to tell her how grateful I was, that she had gone above and beyond, she replied, "I'm just being practical, Jane. After all, who wants to eat macaroni and cheese every day for weeks?"

When she arrived, we spread ourselves out at the dining-room table with Buddy and his squeaky toys at our feet.

"So has Clayton made it past the thirty-day mark yet?" asked Jenn.

I started counting the days in my head. The thirty-day challenge had become a popular buzz phrase people use to describe overcoming obstacles to change. Some people do yoga for thirty consecutive days, others diet, some try to quit smoking, go on the wagon, or do a cleanse. Quite frankly, it is incomprehensible to me, though, why one would put oneself and one's body through something close to a colonoscopy prep every day for thirty days. Nonetheless, according to the lady at the health food store, some people actually do this.

"Yes, he is well past thirty days now."

More importantly, Clayton had endured his own thirty-day challenge. He had: survived a tumultuous seventy-two-hour stay in an emergency room trauma unit, a rocky ten-day stay in the intensive care unit, a nineteen-day stay on a neurosurgical ward, and a twenty-one-day-and-counting stay in the ABI rehabilitation program. And in that time he had improved his mobility and gone from using a walker to walking unassisted, as well as gaining back some long- and short-term memory recall.

Clayton had also taken on the role of floor captain and patient advocate on 3 South. Apparently, he was verbally sparring with the attending physician and staff daily about access to passes, patient rights, and hospital policy and procedures in general. According to Gina, the clinical coordinator, "He hasn't lost his debating skills either."

All kidding aside, I was eternally grateful Clayton was finding his stride and moving forward with his recovery. There seemed to be light at the end of the tunnel and gratitude helped this light shine even brighter.

Jenn passed me my coffee. "So, has the rehab team given you any idea about what's next?"

Like me, Jenn was a consummate planner; she was always thinking ten steps ahead and knew how I thought. That was one of the reasons we were such good friends. While everyone else was on A, we were already thinking about how to make it to Z.

I explained that although the ABI program and its staff were terrific, and I was very grateful to them, right now Clayton's discharge plan was akin to the Cadbury Caramilk secret. The program's policy was to have a team conference with the patient and family a week before discharge. Since the discharge date was not set, there had been no meeting scheduled, and consequently, no straightforward recommendations. Of course as a former strategic planner and very logical thinker, this made no sense.

What I had gleaned via individual conversations with the social worker, physiotherapist, psychologist, and occupational therapist, was that I needed to keep exploring discharge options for Clayton. The staff members were apprehensive, as I was, to have Clayton return home with me during his weekend passes. They were concerned that with his vulnerable memory and strong personality he might refuse to come back to the hospital altogether. Or, that given the layout of our home, he might fall and reinjure himself.

Being the CEO of Everything, I had thankfully found a short-term solution. With help from my good friend Anna, I found a beautiful apartment in a retirement residence close to the house. The dwelling offered respite relief for caregivers, so Clayton and I stayed at the apartment together a couple of weekends to give him a break from his program. While it was not ideal, it was a lovely respite for both of us. The accommodation had enabled us to have some privacy and time together, with extra support from nursing staff to monitor Clayton and his medical needs in a safe environment. Something to express gratitude for.

I looked over at Buddy trying to hop on Jenn's lap as she surfed intently on her cell phone. "What are you doing, Jenn?"

"I'm doing what should have been done weeks ago; I'm ordering Clayton a plaque to celebrate his thirty-day challenge. Then I'm going out to help you shovel your driveway; it's a mess out there and the last thing we need is for you to fall and hit your head."

I laughed out loud. Even though I didn't see her as often as I should, I could always count on Jenn to be there when I needed her, and to help me see the upside of things.

My cell rang. "Hello?"

"Hi, Ms. Enright. It's Margarite from 3 South calling. I just wanted you to know that we've had an elopement. Everyone on the rehabilitation floor is quite upset. If you can, I think you should get down here ASAP."

Gratitude can help us see the upside rather than the downside of situations.

Gratitude can help us develop and maintain a positive perspective while we manoeuvre any kind of change, especially unexpected change.

Dear friends and family,

It was an eventful day on 3 South today; there was a Code Yellow—an elopement.

This does not mean someone got down on one knee, proposed with wild abandon, found an officiant, and got married; that would have been fun to watch. It means a patient was AWOL—Absent Without Leave—from a locked ward.

The word is "Crazy Victor" (I did not name him this; Bobby, C's roommate, did), was MIA: Missing in Action. He made it all the way from the hospital to the top of the mountain brow about ten kilometres away without shoes, identification, money, or a coat. Luckily for him it was a warm March day.

When I arrived Saturday, the nurses were understandably frantic, and the patients were hedging their bets to see how long Victor would be able to elude the authorities. After a few tense hours, police thankfully found him before it got dark and returned him safely to the ward. This event serves to remind us about the vulnerability of brain-injury patients and is another opportunity to demystify the rehabilitation process.

What exactly is the purpose of rehab?
Forrest Gump might say rehab is like a box of chocolates; everyone's injuries are unique, and you never know what you are going to get. I would also add it is also a bit like watching paint peel. In other words, rehab is a very slow, but important process of examining the layers of one's brain function to see what the root cause of the problem is, so you can fix it.

An example of this would be short-term memory. Assessments help determine what tasks are affected, such as attention and concentration, processing, retrieval, and the corresponding area of the brain that might be the root cause. Therapies help address diminished function to help patients return to activities of daily living.

Why is the ward locked?

To look at C and others on 3 South, you might say, "Hey, what's the problem? He/she looks and sounds great." You are right, they do, and many patients make some very solid progress.

However, C, and others like him, cannot fall or re-injure themselves, especially while injuries are healing. This is why patients are closely monitored and kept in a bit of a holding tank for weeks and months so they don't put themselves in harm's way. Discharge strategies emphasize being super-safe, and patients are monitored as necessary.

Thankfully C is making progress with his recovery. However, there is a reason he has been in the hospital for forty-eight days. This injury requires major intervention and support to help him recover. Being in the ABI program is a strategy that is helping C manage his injuries and move forward with the "new normal" and reality of life.

Consequently, all of your visits, cards, emails, offers to help, great food, good wishes, friendship, humour, and support are still very important to help C achieve the best outcomes possible.

Thanks a million to everyone on this list for hanging in there with us for forty-eight days . . . We appreciate everything you have done and still need you—lots!
Love to all . . .
Jane

OMG™

CHAPTER TEN

Crossing to Safety

···

*It is love and friendship, the sanctity
and celebration of our relationships, that not
only support a good life, but create one.*

—WALLACE STEGNER

" I 'm glad they found Crazy Victor."

"Me too, C."

We were walking to a café around the corner from the hospital. The staff had given C a supervised pass so we could go out for lunch together and take a stroll in the sunshine. As of that day, Clayton had survived sixty days at HGH. He had beaten the odds twice, and survived two serious brain injuries. Although we were still waiting for the plaque Jenn had ordered, we needed to celebrate.

"C, look out!" I grasped the back of Clayton's windbreaker and yanked him back to the curb. "Holy Christmas, C, you scared me. You almost got hit!"

"I was just following you, Jane."

Crazy Victor's departure from 3 South had been a sobering event for me. It had made my recent conversations with

Clayton's neurologist, Dr. MacArthur, and the reality of Clayton's injuries hit home for me. While Clayton has tenacity, determination, and strength in spades, he also has, according to Dr. MacArthur and the kid, agnosia and anosognosia.

Agnosia occurs when the brain experiences damage along sensory pathways. These are the parts of the brain that store knowledge and information regarding the identification and perception of things.[14] There are three main types of agnosia: visual, tactile, and auditory. This means that for Clayton his visual system (facial recognition, visual cues), how he hears and processes auditory messages, and his tactile senses (sense of smell and taste), are still upside down, not right side up.

Anosognosia is the inability to perceive the realities of one's own medical condition.[15] The problem is lack of insight and issues with feedback mechanisms in your brain. Anosognosia is common among patients with Clayton's type of brain injury. It can cause compromised thinking, altered perception and judgement, skewed decision-making, and real safety concerns. This is because patients with anosognosia truly believe they are not as sick as others say they are, and this can put them in dangerous situations.[16] For instance, in Crazy Victor's case, there was leaving the hospital in extreme temperatures, without proper attire, and refusing or forgetting to take important medications. In Clayton's case, it manifested with him stepping into traffic without recognizing the stop signal and nearly getting hit by a car. Looking at these incidents from the outside in, I quickly realized it could have just as easily been Clayton, not Crazy Victor, who had gone AWOL.

When we got back to the unit, I told Clayton I was going make a phone call. In reality, I needed some time to myself. I passed Dr. MacArthur on the way to the cafeteria.

14. Healthline.com/what_is_anosognosia
15. wikipedia.org/Wiki/Anosognosia
16. Ibid

He gave me a wave. "How are things going?"

I described the latest traffic mishaps, plus Clayton's reaction.

"Have you had your discharge meeting with the rest of the team yet?"

I shook my head, "No, it's not scheduled for another two weeks."

He looked at his watch, and motioned me towards the cafeteria. "Let's grab a coffee."

When we sat down, I finally asked the question that I had been dreading to ask the ABI team for sixty days. "Dr. MacArthur, given Clayton's injuries, what is his prognosis?"

He smiled empathetically. "There are many unknowns here. What we do know is that brain injuries are not like a broken arm or leg; there is no defined recovery time, only guidelines. Injuries of this magnitude normally take one to two years to heal. Given Clayton's previous injury and age, recovery will be slower, usually double what it normally would take. He has made great progress, and we hope he will continue to improve. However, because of the severity of his injuries, he will always have challenges for the rest of his life."

"What about the anosognosia? Is that ever going to go away?"

"Anosognosia is complicated because it is not stubbornness or denial on the part of the person who has it. Anosognosia occurs because the patient's brain signals are crossed—it is the damaged brain's way of making sense of things. I equate it to feeling like a super-hero; sometimes the patient has an imaginary Superman cape on and they believe they are invincible. Although their behaviour is not conscious or intentional, it is still very stressful for the person on the receiving end of things. It can also be dangerous for the person who has it. Anosognosia is not always constant; but it is still there."

This made a lot of sense. I was behind Clayton when the traffic incident happened, not in front of him. I had been following him; he had not been following me. This was the third time in two weeks he had stepped into traffic during outings. It was also the third time he had not believed there was a problem.

Clayton's health team had witnessed similar behaviour too. Tina, the occupational therapist, had shared that last week Clayton had lost his balance on his weekly outing to the market. Tina had caught him just before he was about hit the concrete. When Clayton and I discussed this together, Clayton had said, "I was fine, J. Tina was the one who lost her balance, not me, I caught her."

This was not the Clayton I knew. The Clayton I knew was accomplished, logical, precise, accurate, and an exceptional problem solver. He also did not step into traffic, or put himself in harm's way.

Sitting with Dr. MacArthur, I stirred my coffee for a long time. "Is there a chance he might make a full recovery?"

I could feel the doctor choosing his words carefully.

"This accident is a life-altering injury for Clayton. This type of event comes with some major life changes and serious responsibilities. The priority has to be safety first and prevention of reinjury. Going from an ultra-protective rehabilitation centre to life in the outside world requires a great deal of assistance and support for continued recovery and the best outcomes possible."

For the past two months, Clayton's life had been analogous to John Travolta's in the movie, *The Boy in the Plastic Bubble*. He had been protected and sheltered so he would not reinjure himself. Clayton could not hit his head, not even a teensy-weensy bit. If he did, he could suffer another bleed and a serious permanent setback—more brain damage or death. Dr. MacArthur had driven that point home to Clayton and me during our last appointment.

Clayton could still walk, talk, carry on a conversation, talk politics and current events, speak French, read, write, analyze, tell a joke, debate you, play billiards, do math, play chess, share stories, and correct my grammar. In many ways he was the same old Clayton—very kind, generous, thoughtful with his actions and words, and endearing. He still remembered buying me flowers every Friday, so he did this when he visited the market with his rehab group. He also still remembered buying me an engagement ring from Tiffany's, but he could not remember one day to the next—so he proposed to me, daily.

Looking at the situation from the inside out, my heart hurt. I still wanted Clayton to be that same man who had me at hello; the one who was the CEO of Everything and told me that he could walk around the world a million times and never find another woman like me. Yet, looking at things from the outside in, I understood that Dr. MacArthur had, in a sense, unlocked the Cadbury Caramilk secret. He was giving me information that up until this point I had not received—keys to informed decision-making.

When I got back to 3 South, Clayton gave me a big hug. "When do you think I'll be able to come home J? When do you think we'll be able to get married?"

I put my head on his shoulder.

In order for Clayton to cross safely into the outside world, I needed to accept that I would have to continue to think and plan for the both of us. In order to do that, I needed to keep doing what I had been doing for the past sixty days: practice outside-in thinking, mindfulness, and gratitude.

> **Outside-in thinking. Mindfulness. Gratitude™**
> OMG™ is a strategy you can use to successfully navigate change and make your ideas happen, so you can land butter-side up in the game of life.

....

Dear friends and family,

As of March 17, C has endured sixty days at HGH. He has beaten the odds and survived two serious brain injuries. To put this accomplishment into context, I'd like to bring you back to my previous conversations fifty days ago with four neurosurgeons, plus the kid, when I asked:

"On a scale of 1–7, with 7 being the most serious ever, and 1 being not serious at all, how serious is this injury?" Independently, each one gave me the same number: 5. This accident is a life-altering injury for C, so in the words of his healthcare team, this event comes with some serious life changes and some serious responsibilities. The priority has to be safety first, and prevention of reinjury. Therefore, going from ultra-protective rehab to life in the outside world requires a lot of assistance to support continued recovery and the best outcomes possible.

I know reading this you must have questions, so let's have FAQ Time:

What is the likelihood of recovery for an ABI patient?
Several factors determine the likelihood of a strong recovery, or not, from an Acquired Brain Injury. A previous injury makes recovery from subsequent injuries longer and more difficult, as does an increase in one's age and the severity of the injury. Unfortunately for C, he has had a previous TBI, a bleed in his brain and moderate head injury when he had his bike accident: strike one. His second TBI is more severe with a major bleed and includes a fractured skull: strike two. He is also older than most patients: strike three.

Will C be able to do everything he used to do?
The short answer is yes and no.

C's life has changed, and will continue to change;
when you hit your head like this you cannot expect
everything to be business as usual. In other words,
we have choices in life, but sometimes, depending on
circumstances beyond our control, choices are made
for you. For example:

Driving
C will not be able to drive. When you have an injury
as severe as this, your licence is suspended for medical
reasons. This is a major loss of independence for
anyone. Also, because of his injury he cannot just hop
on a commuter train or grab a cab, right now he has
too many memory issues.

Working
C has been advised not to return to work right now—
his brain needs more time to heal. This is very hard for
a man whose life has mostly been his work. When he
is ready, C is hoping to resume research and writing
on his favourite book topics, but the jury is still out
on any other work-related activities.

Housing
For medical reasons, C is not able to return home
right now. He requires more support and assistance
to manage his injuries than I can provide. Even if
renovations were made to the house, this would not
guarantee his physical safety. Hence the healthcare
team has recommended assisted living as a bridge now
between a locked ward, home, and the outside world.

Is all of this tough? You bet. This event is a casserole of unplanned change for both of us, and a lot to adjust to. Nonetheless, if C does not change his lifestyle and adapt his surroundings, the likelihood he will progress with his recovery and not reinjure himself is minimal. Right now, he has the odds stacked against him; he needs to have every opportunity possible to have the best outcomes possible.

So what's the plan?
Given the medical recommendations, C and I have been working with the healthcare team to put together a transition and recovery plan. We stayed at a care residence apartment in March on the weekends to give C a break from rehab; it was lovely and we both really enjoyed it. Given the doctor's advice and safety concerns, this is C's bridge to independence.

Starting in April, we will rent a one-bedroom suite at the retirement residence. It is safe, beautiful, and will give C the support and assistance he needs to get stronger and continue his rehab so he can have the best outcomes possible. Services such as physiotherapy, speech-pathology, and occupational therapy will come to C, not the other way around. This will make it far easier for him to rest and recover, receive the support he needs in a timely manner, and have a great quality of life.

I will stay with him when I can, support my children to finish their graduation years at home, and work when I can. When I cannot be physically present with him, C will have the assistance he needs to manage his injuries. The good news is that this is not your average retirement residence—it is like staying at the Ritz Carlton, which C is very familiar with. There is an abundance of medical staff and activities to keep him engaged and involved. When he is ready, C will have the independence to walk downtown to a variety of shops and services without having to rely on me all the time for a ride.

I am sure reading this has been a lot to absorb. It has been a lot for me to absorb too, and of course, a lot to explain to everyone. That's why I had to wait to write to all of you. I needed time to process what is happening.

Save the date
Once C is settled in, we are planning to have a party to show you the new place and thank everyone for their support and kindness. My hope is that you will attend and continue to support C as you always have, by visiting him at the condo and providing your friendship to him. "It takes a village" rings true, and we are still going to need you—lots! Please know we both sincerely appreciate everything everyone has done and are so thankful for your support.

The next few weeks will be busy with discharge plans and moving, but I promise to keep in touch and look forward to seeing everyone soon to thank you in person for your kindness.

Until then, please remember, don't count the days; make the days count!

Love to all and thanks for hanging in with us for seventy-six days . . .
Best, Jane

CHAPTER ELEVEN

The Third Thing

··

Little by little we let go of grief,
but never of love.

—ANONYMOUS

The party I was planning to thank everyone never happened. Mere weeks after helping me shovel my driveway, and five days after my last email update, Jenn was diagnosed with stage-four cancer. She arrived at the ER complaining of abdominal pain and left with the worst news of her life.

People say they remember what they were doing when Kennedy was shot. Similarly, I will never forget where I was when I received this news. It was late afternoon on a Saturday, and I was sitting in my favourite chair. I received a telephone call from Jenn's sister-in-law, who said Jenn wanted me to know about her diagnosis and had wanted to tell me herself, but she couldn't. She knew I had just spent months helping Clayton in the hospital with his journey, and she did not want to burden me with hers. That's Jenn, she was selfless.

After hanging up the phone, I sobbed and shook uncontrollably. My eighteen-year-old son ran downstairs when he heard me crying. He took one look at me, immediately cancelled his Saturday night party plans, and hugged me tight until I could get the words out to tell him what was happening. Finally, after no more tears could come from me, he looked at me, smiled gently, and said, "Mom, do you want to watch *Ferris Bueller's Day Off* together tonight?"

March 24, 2018, was one of the worst days of my life and one of the best. It was the worst because I knew what lay ahead for my friend. She was not going to celebrate her next wedding anniversary. Nor was she going to see her children graduate or marry. She would never hug her grandchildren. Yet, I also experienced firsthand what my younger son Ryan was made of. He confirmed I had raised a compassionate, empathetic child who knew how to make good choices and had the capability of doing the right thing at the right time.

Growing up, Jenn didn't know right away whether she wanted kids. One day, when we were about thirteen, hanging out at the mall, we saw a very frazzled mother with four kids under the age of about seven. Jenn turned to me, as only she could, and said very emphatically, "I'm never doing that. You can't feed four kids on two t_ts!" We laughed so hard together, and we continued to laugh together for the next forty years.

The morning after I received the news, I tried to call Jenn, but I couldn't speak. I knew I wanted to do something, but I literally had no voice. I knew I wanted to reach out and comfort her, but I also knew I had to do it in a way that would give her strength and hope, and not share my inner feelings of sadness and despair. So, I did what I had been doing for seventy-six days; I started to write.

Not everyone gets to have a best friend for forty years, moreover, someone as special, kind, and wonderful as Jennifer Jean. They broke the mold when they made her. As I wrote my message to Jenn, I experienced a plethora of emotions. Those emotions included anger and helplessness, and confusion over why this was happening—especially now. Most of all, I felt love for my treasured friend and gratitude for our friendship, which had lasted forty years, much longer than most marriages.

After the shock wore off, I realized I had learned from experience that unexpected change can occur rapidly, at any moment. That realization also helped me accept, rather quickly, what was happening. Looking at this situation from the outside in, I understood like C, Jenn was going to need an advocate. I was also mindful the clock was ticking, and that we didn't have much time. I was neither happy nor grateful for this new change, but I was happy and grateful for the wonderful gift of her friendship for forty years.

It was while reflecting and writing to Jenn that I really pulled all my lessons together, my OMG; Outside-in Thinking, Mindfulness and Gratitude It was OMG that helped me carry on, carry forward, help myself, and help my friend after one of the worst days of my life.

We are all faced with situations in our lives, especially ones that involve grief and loss, where there seems to be nothing to be grateful for. During those moments it can be very difficult to stay grounded, know what to say to others, or how to say it. My hope is that by sharing my experience, and a personal piece of correspondence, it will help you dig deep to find and express your gratitude and love, and help your loved one and yourself through a difficult situation.

> Acceptance and OMG are your friends in a tough situation.
> They are tools that can help you find strength and courage to hang on when all you want to do is let go and let go when all you want to do is hang on. Outside-in thinking. Mindfulness. Gratitude.

....

Dearest Jenn,

I should be calling you and Rob right now and putting on my best face and voice, but I am so emotional I can't speak or find the words I need to tell you what I want to say.

Where do I begin to tell you how much you mean to me, what a wonderful friend and important influence you are in my life, and how devastated I am about your diagnosis and that this is even happening? I can't even imagine how you, Rob, Brent, Evan, and your family must be feeling. This must be such a shock and so emotionally and physically draining. If I could take this all away for you, I would, in a heartbeat. I love you so much, Jenn, and never want you to suffer in any way.

Bottom line: This is not fair and it sucks with a capital f*&!%** S.

Jenn, we have shared the best of times and the worst of times. You and I have been through so much together. You have always given me the strength, the drive, and the determination to carry on and forward through the toughest times of my life. Now it is my turn to give you my love, warmth, friendship, and strength. Yes, I do have a lot going on in my life, but never so much that I can't be there for you, Rob, the kids, and your parents, and I mean big time.

I know you have a lot ahead of you, and I want to help you make every moment count, not count the days. I want your bucket list, and I want to help you make it happen. Everything from I want a piece of chocolate fudge cake today to let's fly to Vegas tomorrow—I am not kidding. I want to help you seize the day, your way, anyway you want to, when you want to. I sincerely mean that. I need a couple of days to get my s&%! together and get C moved to his new place. Then let's get going and kick some ass in the I'm-going-to-make-the-most-of-what-I-can-everyday department.

When you can, please let me know the best way to reach you and when the best time is to visit. I want to give you the biggest hug ever! Call me or text me any time of day or night . . . I mean that. I am here for you and here to help you and Rob make things happen when you need and want to.

BTW: You still owe me a boozy lunch. Just because you are sick doesn't mean I am letting you off the hook for our annual Boozy Birthday lunch date.

Love and biggest hugs ever . . . J

P.S. To help manage expectations, please remember, we can make a lot of things happen, but we can't feed four kids on two t—ts.

Unfortunately, Jenn and I never got to have that boozy birthday lunch together. She called me from her hospital bed late one afternoon. It was the second week of April, only two and a half weeks since her diagnosis.

She said, very emphatically, "Do you know where I am?"

Morphine had played with her sense of space and time, but not with her spirit. Jenn told me she knew she didn't have much longer, and that she wanted me to return to the hospital right away to be with her until the end. And I was, each day and every day, until she passed away a few days later.

When I saw Jenn for the last time, she wasn't conscious, but I knew she could hear me. I told her *that it was not goodbye for us; rather, it was bon voyage. I told her that she would be in my heart, each and every day, at the top of Beaver Valley Ski Club, getting ready for another run down the hill together.*

Race ya my friend!
XO Love J

....

OMG:
Am I
Butter
Side Up
Yet?

CHAPTER TWELVE

Changes and Corrections

···

"It's only after we've lost everything,
we're free to do anything."
—CHUCK PALAHNIUK

The days, weeks, and months after C's discharge and Jenn's death were a complete blur for me.

Simultaneously, I was grieving the loss of my best girlfriend, supporting her family, supervising a team of healthcare providers for Clayton, working with lawyers to settle Clayton's and my personal injury claims, trying to keep my career afloat, saying goodbye to my sons as they moved thousands of miles away, and, along with Buddy, adjusting to being an empty nester. To complicate matters, I was still experiencing symptoms from my own head injury, including painful headaches I thought I had conquered. Three months after one hundred days in the hospital, I was still the CEO of Everything, managing just about everything.

"Okay everyone, you have ten more minutes to lie on your mat in Savasana. The light in me, bows to the light in you . . . namaste."

In the midst of all this I was attempting to carve out some time for myself with something I had taken up years before: yoga. After Clayton's accident, I made a conscious decision to try and take a class between hospital visits—not to sit on the couch, drink wine, and eat chips. Thankfully the former, not the latter, usually won out, and I lost eighteen pounds during his hospital stay. Moreover, the time I reserved for myself kept me mindful and helped me make some new friends. The studio where I practiced became a welcome refuge from the chaos in my life. As I was coming out of the change room one day, Emily, the instructor, flagged me down.

"Hey Jane, great to see you! I was just wondering . . . are you interested in going on that retreat with us? I have one spot left."

A couple of months prior, Emily had noticed me looking at a poster for a yoga retreat in Italy. I had backpacked through Europe in my early twenties, and Italy had been a favourite destination of mine. The retreat was a week at a farmhouse in the beautiful Sabine hills outside Rome; it looked amazing.

"Oh wow, I thought it was scheduled for next year? When is it?"

"It's this summer, in just over a month."

I looked at the dates on the poster. It was at the same time I had been trying to organize a trip for Clayton and me. We both loved the beach, and at Clayton's discharge meeting, his physiatrist agreed a short flight and some rest and relaxation seaside would be okay. Clayton and I were both excited at the prospect of travelling again, but we needed Dr. MacArthur's consent too.

Ironically, and I don't think by coincidence, Dr. MacArthur was the physician assigned for my own neurological follow-up later that day at the concussion clinic at the hospital. When I explained to him all the things that I was responsible for, and that I seemed to be going backwards, instead of forwards, he surprised me when he said, "That's because you are, Jane."

Dr. MacArthur explained that just like a car has a reserve gas tank for emergencies, so do our brains. And, when one gets hit in the head with such a force as I did, not only do all the files get spilled on the floor, your brain loses its capacity to tap into those reserves, especially under stress. In a nutshell, the accident had put my brain at a disadvantage, and all this stress with a capital %#$*&@! S, had made it worse. My headaches, short term memory challenges, and speech aphasia—difficulty speaking clearly, were symptoms of my brain overtaxed by stress compounded by my accident.

"Are my symptoms ever going to go away? Am I ever going to go forward again?"

He looked at me seriously. "When you experience these symptoms, it's because your brain's reserve tank is on empty, not full. You are fifty-one years old, not twenty-one years old Jane, and still recovering from a serious injury. Given that it has been well over a year since your accident and you still have symptoms, it's likely you will always have to manage your injuries in some capacity. Moving forward, the breadth, depth, and severity of those symptoms will be proportional to your environment and how you manage it. How you choose to move ahead and manage your life will influence and determine if you move forwards or backwards with your recovery. Keeping that tank in your brain filled, not empty, will be crucial for you to achieve the best outcomes possible for yourself.

His pager went off. "We're going to have wrap this up, but you're coming in tomorrow with Clayton, right? My assistant mentioned you have some forms you wanted me to sign?"

"Yes. Clayton's physiatrist said she thought a short holiday would be okay. She felt that we should clear it through you, though. We also have some forms that need to be signed for C's health insurance."

He raised his eyebrows, and then searched through some papers on his desk. "Ahh, here it is—Clayton's lab work and vitals just came in this morning. Looking at this, three months post-discharge, his blood pressure is still unstable and his sodium levels are low. This is probably what has been giving him those dizzy spells. In my opinion, he needs more tests and an endocrinology assessment. Given his current condition and risk of falling, I'm sorry, but I cannot approve any sort of travel right now. If I did, he would be at risk of reinjury, and you would be at risk of losing your house—the insurance company is not going to cover a hospital visit because of his pre-conditions. At best, I think you are going to have to wait for at least a year for things to stabilize. I'm sorry I couldn't be more helpful."

After the appointment, I walked down to the café where Clayton and I used to go to for our favourite soup. Sitting in that exam room I felt like I was in the principal's office again, only this time I wasn't receiving a reprimand, I was receiving a wake-up call about my life.

While I had been on autopilot taking care of everyone else, I had underestimated the impact of my own accident and the toll this unplanned change had taken on my own health. I had been looking at Clayton's life from the outside in, but looking at my own life from the inside out. In doing so, I had calculated the future impact of C's injuries on his life, yet miscalculated the impact of his injuries on mine.

As I was finishing lunch, my cell rang. It was Denise, the director of nursing from the retirement home.

"Hi Denise, how are you? Is everything okay?"

"I just wanted to let you know we tried to come into the apartment this morning to take Clayton's blood pressure and ensure he took his meds. He barricaded the door with a chair again and won't let us in."

I was visiting Clayton almost daily, and he was coming home for dinners and visits, but he still needed monitoring. Thankfully he had weekly visits from his physiotherapist, speech, and occupational therapists to assist him with his rehabilitation plan. Plus, he had activities and outings to help keep his keen mind stimulated. Nonetheless, the biggest challenge was that with his anosognosia, he didn't always understand that he required medication or assistance from others.

This included steadfastly refusing to have anyone at home to help us when he was there; he told me flat out that he didn't "need to be babysat." I knew deep down that when these outbursts happened, it wasn't the Clayton I knew, and that he wasn't purposely being difficult. He was just trying, in his own way, to be the CEO of Everything like he used to be.

The hardest part was that if I was honest with myself and looked at this situation, and my own life, from the outside in, instead of the inside out, I had to accept things had been difficult for both of us for a long time. There had been changes with Clayton after the first accident. Changes that not only I had seen, but others had seen as well. Personality shifts that most likely were the result of his first head injury and beyond his control, yet difficult for the two of us all the same. We had been going to counselling, discussing how to move forward, and considering separation, when his second accident happened.

Reflecting, I realized that in twelve months I had lost everything I knew was so: my partner, my best friend Jenn, my career, and, temporarily, my children. Now, according to Dr. MacArthur, I was also in jeopardy of losing my own health, for good. Even though I was trying hard to land butter-side up, in reality, I was still butter-side down in a place that was brimming with lots of trauma and drama; a place where I knew I did not want to be anymore but wasn't sure how to move away from. Nonetheless, I did understand that if something didn't change in my life soon, I would be the one in the soup, and no good to anyone.

"Thanks for calling, Denise. I'm so sorry this has happened. Please tell C that I am on my way."

When I hung up, I did something that I didn't expect to do. I called Emily and told her I was going to Italy.

As I was preparing to leave, I realized, although I had been on many business trips by myself, I had never actually taken a vacation on my own. Except for a few yoga classes with Emily, I didn't know a soul before I went on that trip. Boarding that flight for Italy was scary and exciting all at the same time, and that leap of faith turned out to be one of the best decisions I ever made.

In beautiful Sabina, Italy, I got to focus just on me. For an entire week I was reminded of what life could be like butter-side up, instead of butter-side down. I didn't worry about the past or anticipate the future; I was mindful and focused on the present. I took each day and wonderful experience as it came and had tons of fun with a great bunch of girls. When I told my Sabina sisters how much I had enjoyed the retreat, and how happy and grateful I was to share this experience together, my new friend Diane said it best when she replied, "It's amazing what a little normal can do."

While I did not make any final decisions about my relationship with Clayton during that time away, I did initiate more planned change. I consciously decided that in order to successfully move forward, not backward, I needed to take care of myself first, to do a scan of my own life, and determine what I needed and wanted to live a joyous, happy life. I knew from my conversation with my neurologist that I needed to reduce stress and the responsibilities in my life. However, it wasn't until the fall (I call it my tower moment) that I realized what I ultimately had to do.

It was at the end of October 2018, on a cold, very windy, almost snowy day. Clayton and I were at the house together with my parents, who had flown in from the West Coast for a visit. We were sitting in the dining room having lunch when Clayton announced, "J, I'm going to paint the house."

I looked at him in surprise. "Do you mean you want to paint the inside of the house C, or the outside, C?" "The outside. It's looking worn and needs to be painted."

My parents and I looked at each other and bit our lips. Because I knew how C's mind worked, or how it used to, I tried to talk him through his thinking by looking at things from the outside-in, as an observer rather than a participant. "C, how will you paint the outside of the house? How do you want to make this happen?"

"Well, because I can't drive right now, you can go to the store and buy the paint and the supplies. Considering you are the one that is good with colours, you can choose any colour you want. Then when you get home, I'll get up on the ladder and paint the house."

That's when my mother piped up and said, "C, I'm not sure Dr. MacArthur would want you to climb a ladder propped against a two-story home to do that."

"Sheila, Dr. MacArthur is a moron and incompetent. I can do anything I want."

I chose my words carefully. "C, I think it's great you want to paint the house, but how will you paint the upper story? It's very high up there."

"I'll climb out the window, stand on the roof, and paint."

When I gently tried to remind him that we had hired a professional to paint the house before, he replied, "J, I know what I'm doing. I'm not paying a professional to do something I can do myself."

Conversing with him, trying to make sense of something that made no sense, I realized this situation was never going to change. Thankfully, I was at home that day when Clayton decided he wanted to paint the house, but what if I hadn't been? Or, what if I was, and was on the phone, or doing laundry, when he decided to go up the ladder? This was not the first time a similar situation had occurred; I had witnessed

Clayton climbing onto a ladder in the garage several times since his discharge. Also, lifting heavy objects and climbing stairs, putting him at risk of stumbling and falling. Paired with these episodes was the subsequent tension that followed between us. His latest idea to paint the house was just the tipping point for me that brought forth the reality, risks, and emotional turmoil of the situation.

Blissfully, Clayton could not remember recovering from his first accident. Unfortunately, I could. We had been down this road before and consulted far more neurosurgeons and neurologists than one should in a lifetime. I understood and accepted what lay ahead for him: that his challenges would be difficult, even more so, this time around. It was at that moment I finally accepted that if we remained a couple, living together or apart, my life would be more difficult, even more so, too. In doing so, I would be at risk of becoming resentful for my life, not grateful for it as I should be. I had to face my fears and make a choice between having a comfortable, peaceful life or settling for an uncomfortably comfortable one.

When we are looking for happiness, we often look to others to make us happy. We expect situations and other people to change. However, we cannot change others, control their behaviour, circumstances, choices, or decisions. We can only control our own reactions and our own choices, which ultimately change us.

I believe choosing happiness and creating more of it, is an act of conscious will. Our perspective impacts our thoughts, moods, and daily life, and helps us manage our external world. It is our responsibility to shift our perspective from negative to positive; to define what we want our life to look like; and to cultivate a solid life plan to make it happen. In other words, happiness is a choice; one that we make moment to moment, day by day. Once you accept this, you don't find happiness—you create it. Happiness is an inside job.

In December, when my sons couldn't come home for the holidays, I went to visit them in Banff, Alberta. When I told them my decision, they accepted it, and they shared that moving forward, they wanted both Clayton and me to have the best life possible. They also announced their work visas for Australia had been approved, which would take them away for another year. I told them I would miss them terribly and wanted to visit, but couldn't envision right now how I would travel so far on my own.

That's when my older son Ross surprised me with one of the kindest, heartfelt gifts I have ever received when he said: "Mom, why don't you join us on our trip? Why don't you come along and drop us off?"

> I believe you don't find happiness; you create it. OMG can help you take responsibility for choices that can help you land butter-side up in the game of life.

Dearest C,

I have probably written you hundreds of pieces of correspondence over our time together, but none as challenging, heartfelt, or as sincere as this one.

I want to thank you for all the joy, love, warmth, and abundance you have brought to my life, our life, and my children's lives. Throughout our years together you have always believed, encouraged, and supported me to the moon and back, oftentimes when I did not, or could not, recognize my own capabilities or encourage myself to be the very best that I could be. I truly do not believe I would have become the person

I am today without you or the experiences I have shared with you. For that, I am eternally grateful.

To say we have been through a lot would be the understatement of the year. I would equate our years together as going through Dieppe, Vimy Ridge, and Normandy all at the same time. At the end of the day, some might not call us partners, but war buddies. We have shared the best of times and the worst of times. Yet I know if we were sitting together talking about our relationship, we would both say it was so much more than that.

I have given you everything I have, C, to ensure you can have the best life and outcomes possible; not only after your first accident, but after your most recent one too. I know you have given me everything you have to give too. Nonetheless, if I am truly honest with myself about our state of affairs, I have to accept that I cannot give you the lifetime commitment of marriage you truly deserve and desire. This is not because I don't love you or care about you and your well being; it is quite the opposite. I know in my heart I cannot go the distance—that in order for me to move forward, not backward, I cannot fulfill your hopes, dreams, desires, as well as mine at the same time.

We have survived and endured the most incredible storyline together, C; no one could have scripted or predicted it. In the end, I am so very sorry this choice had to be made. I am hopeful that someday you will be able to accept this. Moving forward, my wish is that one day you might be able to welcome me into your life as a supporting actress, rather than the lead one.
Love always,
SJ

OMG: What's Next?

CHAPTER THIRTEEN

Making Sense of it All

*"In the end only three things matter;
how much you loved, how gently you
lived, and how gracefully you let go of
things not meant for you."*

—BUDDHA

After my most terrible year, I intentionally started changing my perspective and my mindset. I believe you are what you believe and that the majority of us have the ability to create a new reality for ourselves. I also understand that most people, either by circumstance, such as a lack of know-how, or by choice, don't take time to envision what it is they truly want or need to have a super-awesome life. Nor do they recognize the importance of doing so.

Envisioning what's next after unplanned change that has involved any kind of trauma can be very challenging. This is because it is common for us to become defined, or labelled, by our previous experiences: I am a widower, I am a divorcee, I am unemployed, etc. This thinking, combined with fear of the unknown, can lead to a cycle of predictability and falling into a pattern of rewriting the same chapter of our lives over and over again. Consequently, we become a receiver, not the quarterback, of our life. Rather than making things happen, we let things happen, avoiding change rather than embracing it. The good news is: shifting our perspective can help us change our habits and enable us to write a new and improved storyline for ourselves.

It was OMG (Outside-in Thinking, Mindfulness, Gratitude), believing in myself, and faith that helped me begin to shift my perspective to a more positive mindset and create my new storyline. The first step was embracing planned change and accepting that I wanted things to be different. I started looking outside-in at my own life to determine what I didn't want, so I could create what I did want. I decided I was tired of things that were hard and sad, and that I wanted my life to be the opposite of that. So, on my fifty-second birthday, I self-declared it was going to be my super-awesome year. I really didn't know what I was going to do; I just knew the year was going to be all about me enjoying happy, fun, joyful experiences.

The second step was allowing myself time and space to do that. Consequently, accepting my children's invitation to come along and "drop them off" in Australia morphed into a two-month vacation together to San Francisco; Oahu, Hawaii; New Zealand; Fiji; and Australia. That trip was the ultimate mindfulness journey, or as they say in yoga, one big, long Savasana. Never have I woken up each morning with such joy and anticipation about life. Every day I was in the moment, experiencing a new adventure, creating memories with my children that will last a lifetime. It was during that trip that I began to write about our travels together with the idea that I would assemble a collection of stories about our adventures. Being diligently mindful and writing about my daily experiences supported me to visualize what I wanted the rest of my life to look like, and moreover what it could look like.

Visualization is essentially using your imagination. It is a dress rehearsal in your mind for what comes next. Research has shown that when done well, visualization techniques can help individuals improve how they feel and move forward towards their goals, which is essentially successfully navigating change.[17] Olympic and professional athletes are perfect examples of this; they have been using visualization to see, believe, and achieve success for decades. High achievers such as Olympians envision and plan the route, utilize supports to tackle obstacles along the way, and harness the energy that accomplishment brings to take it to the finish line.[18]

However, what most people fail to grasp, is that to be effective at visualization, just seeing what you want to happen in your life is not enough. You have to have faith and to truly believe and feel what you want to happen actually can happen. The more details you can visualize about your goal or desire, the more real it will seem.[19] When this occurs, your brain's natural problem-solving processes go to work to help you develop a plan to successfully obtain what you want.[20]

Imagining success is more natural for some than others. Children, because of their innocence, have unlimited capability to visualize and believe. Until someone plants a seed in a child's head and tells them they cannot do something, they naturally believe they can do anything. In my case, I have always had a very vivid imagination. As a child I would create scenarios in my mind about what I wanted to experience. I easily pictured myself doing many fun things, including being like Farrah Fawcett, modelling holiday dresses for the

17. Vilhauer, Jennice, "Living Forward: 3 Effective Visualization Techniques to Change Your Life", *Psychology Today*, June 30, 2018
18. Harrison, Melinda, "Personal Next: What We Can Learn From Elite Athletes Navigating Career Transition", Lifetree Publishing 2020
19. Ibid
20. Ibid

Sears Christmas catalogue. When I consciously became more mindful during my time away with my sons, I felt it easy to return to this creative, playful way of thinking. This in turn, supported me towards achieving a more positive mindset.

Nonetheless, unplanned change with unpleasant circumstances can often interfere with our imaginations and our ability to focus on positive thoughts, rather than negative ones. This is because as humans, we are programmed to feel rather than think our way through life. There is a direct link between our thoughts, feelings, reactions, and actions.[21] If we experience something negative, then we are likely to feel negative in some way. In contrast, if something positive happens, then we are likely to think positive thoughts, and feel positive as a result.

Understanding the link between your thoughts, feelings, reactions, and actions is important when you are deciding what comes next after unplanned change. Outside-in thinking can help you take the emotionality out of situations, so you can find clarity of thought. Moreover, mindfulness can calm your mind and support you to respond wisely to events rather than reacting to them. This is where tools such as a vision board or meditation can be very useful in organizing your thoughts and can help kick-start start your imagination and your mindset in a more positive direction. In turn, this can help you move forward and make things happen, instead of letting them happen.

When making choices after unplanned change, it can also be difficult to balance your heart and your head. Your head may be pointing you in one direction (logic and reasoning), and your heart (what you feel) in another. Trusting your intuition (what you feel) sometimes means going against the grain and doing what feels right, rather than what we have

---

21. University of Michigan Depression Centre, 2020; classroommentalhealth.org/thoughts

been taught to do or what others are telling us to do. Positive new beginnings and successfully stickhandling the unexpected often require tapping into both—using logic and trusting your intuition, plus having faith that everything will work out as it should.

My desire to create a website to help inspire and support others to handle the unexpected was a combination of just that: blending business experience and knowledge about how to handle change (logic), with a strong desire to help others do so successfully (feeling), with the belief that I could do it (faith). Some would say it was totally illogical to think I could turn a bunch of emails, a short story, and a travel blog into a website. Faith is believing in miracles when logic tells you not to. Nonetheless, I really took a leap of faith when I began to consider writing a book about my most terrible year. Yet, I had whispers of encouragement and intuition to believe that I could do this which I could not ignore.

The first was in 2017 when I was forced to write when I could not speak properly after my head injury. The emphasis on writing, rather than speaking, helped me sharpen my creative writing skills. Along the way there was encouragement from colleagues, friends, and family that my Dear Friends & Family emails, although sad and tragic, were entertaining and had been enjoyed; people wanted to read more. Second, was an invitation from the Beaver Valley Ski Club (BVSC) in late 2018 to write a memoriam about Jenn for their newsletter. A four-line remembrance quickly turned into a narrative about gratitude for our friendship—which subsequently received great reviews from staff and members. This encouragement prompted me to start envisioning writing a book to help individuals deal with grief and loss.

The tipping point towards turning believing into reality was a powerful chance encounter during a return trip to Italy in 2019 amid my super-awesome year. Before dropping off my children in Australia I had signed up for a second yoga retreat with Emily in Sicily, Italy. One of my favourite destinations there was the town of Modica, home of baroque architecture, the world's first chocolate makers, and my Sicilian miracle at the ORO Hotel.

You must understand that while travelling in Italy you are often hard pressed to find restrooms, let alone toilets with seats, or toilet paper. If you happen to find all three together well, that is a Sicilian miracle. My Sicilian miracle was sort of related, but of a different sort. As I was searching for a restroom and coming up short, I decided that a hotel might be a good place to go. That's when I found myself standing in front of the lovely ORO Hotel in Modica asking to use the ladies room. After the hostess kindly agreed to let me use their pristine bathroom, I decided that it was time to get away from the 35-degree heat and started chatting in broken Italian with the manager. To help each other understand one another we started Google translating our conversation. I shared that I wanted to write about the ORO Hotel on a website I wanted to create. It was then that Katia, the manager, very excitedly pointed to the rows and rows of bookshelves located in the hotel dining room.

"This is a very special place", she Googled back in Italian; it is a place where authors come to dine and leave a signed copy of their book for patrons to look at. We have been doing this for years and many famous authors have come to us. Our collection is housed in our library upstairs. When you write your book will you please come back and provide us with a copy?" In a case of lost in translation, I had mistakenly been taken for an established author and extended an invitation to sign and share my book with patrons; a book still in my imagination and not yet started.

At that moment time stopped for me. I cannot explain the feeling I experienced other than to say it was a strong intuitive spiritual experience—a whisper I could not ignore. Although writing a book, and writing a review on a website had become lost in translation, I clearly understood the reason I had been brought to the ORO Hotel. It was a sign I was on the right track; that I was destined to write the book I had been contemplating and return with it to Italy.

Next, was returning home and volunteering in a kindergarten classroom where I met a wonderful little boy, Adesh, who discovered the power of believing right before my eyes. Adesh inspired me to write my first short story entitled All I Need To Know I Learned In Kindergarten . . . and at The Flower Shop, which led to a happenstance meeting with a publisher.

After a year of uncoupling with Clayton I had, with the urging of friends, registered for a matchmaking site. Did I do this enthusiastically? NO! Truth be told I avoid all things online whenever I can—this includes shopping, social media, and dating. Quite frankly the thought of meeting a new love interest via the internet terrified me. However, I knew that if I was going to begin moving forward with my life, make new friends, and eventually find a new partner, I needed to think outside-in, instead of inside out, so I could move past my fears and be more open to change in that department.

One evening, with Jenn on my shoulder for moral support, I found myself creating a dating profile including my personal interests which at the time were focused on film and film promotion. I made absolutely no mention of my budding interest in writing. No one was more stunned than me when two weeks later while attending the Toronto International Film Festival, (TIFF), I received a message on eharmony from a guy who was a publisher. What are the chances of that?

I cautiously accepted his invitation to meet him for coffee on a Sunday afternoon. After learning I liked to write, my date asked me if I had ever published anything. Coincidentally, (some might call it divine timing), I had just put the finishing touches on my story about Adesh and the flower shop.

"Can I have a read", he asked?

I reluctantly forwarded him the story on my cellphone and then promptly excused myself to grab another coffee while he read it. To be honest, I was nervous about rejection—I did not want to watch him read what I had written. I returned to our table to find him laughing out loud. He smiled and said, "You have a wonderful writing style. Have you ever considered writing more, maybe telling your story about what you just told me?"

To which I replied, "I can't even imagine where I would begin."

All of a sudden that coffee date turned into a two-hour business meeting with priceless advice about the business of publishing, how one might approach writing a book, and publishing one. Although I never did see my publisher friend again, this is advice which I am eternally grateful for.

The third step in designing my new storyline was looking at my life with more gratitude than ever before. There is a quote by author William Bridges that every end is a new beginning.[22] Embracing that philosophy, instead of looking at everything I lost, I started looking at everything I gained. Practicing gratitude daily, I discovered my experiences had taught me lessons that were not only helpful to me but might be useful to others. I recognized that my most terrible year had given me a wonderful gift: a chance to change absolutely everything in my life. My mindset, career, relationships, and my lifestyle—a total redo.

Outside-in thinking helped me visualize and plan the route; mindfulness supported me to navigate the journey; and gratitude illuminated the path. Had it not been for my most

22. Bridges, William, PH.D. *Transitions: Making Sense of Life's Changes*, Da Capo Press, 2004

terrible year, I would not have contemplated taking a trip around the world with my children, volunteered in a classroom, dated on-line, started a new company, or considered writing a book to share my story to help others create *their* super-awesome life.

Unplanned change and OMG opened up my mind to new possibilities and new ways of thinking; so much so, that by the end of my adventures I decided to hell with a super-awesome year; I wanted a super-awesome life! In the end, it was OMG; trusting, not ignoring my intuition; believing in myself; and having faith that everything would be okay that helped me successfully navigate change. I made my ideas happen and created a super-awesome new chapter, which I am happily enjoying today. However, I am the first one to tell you—it takes work!

When we go through unplanned change with lots of trauma and drama, it is hard not to be defined by it. Nonetheless, if you accept and believe that all of us have choices and deserve to be happy, you begin to live life more intentionally. You become more careful of what you let in, and do not let in, to your life, open your mind up to new possibilities, and refuse to be labelled by your circumstances. This is when your past becomes a chapter, not the whole book.

I am an ordinary person who has survived some extraordinary things. I chose to share my experiences to help inspire and encourage you—with a healthy dose of humour along the way—to successfully embrace and navigate change, not fear it. I wanted to tell you my story and share my ideas to help you move forward, not backward, so you can create *your* new storyline, make your ideas happen, and land butter-side up in the game of life. I chose to show you those things because I believe in you. Now it's your turn to believe in yourself.

> Outside-in thinking helps you visualize and plan the route.
>
> Mindfulness supports the journey.
>
> Gratitude illuminates the path.
>
> Outside-in thinking. Mindfulness. Gratitude™

....

Dear friends and family,

Well, I arrived at Pearson airport to start my super-awesome trip and things are going as usual— long line-ups, Air Canada changes my flight because of the 737 crisis, cranky people, arduous customs clearance, no sleep, you know—the usual travel stuff. Everything is going according to Hoyle. However, before I left the house, I have told myself that no matter what happens, this is going to be a super awesome adventure!

I am shoulder to shoulder with hundreds of early-morning passengers waiting in their zones; however, I don't know what zone I am in. I have lost my boarding pass while waiting over an hour to get a coffee and a bagel. Everyone is, of course, giving me the evil eye as I push through the crowd to the desk— there's no way I am missing this flight or space for my carefully packed carry-on bags. I need my boarding pass and my seat.

I arrive at the kiosk and ask the flight attendant where I am sitting; being delightfully ditzy, I can't remember. I think it is in row 8, a seat with some extra legroom. That's when the purser tells me my seat has been reassigned. Now, of course I am ready to give him an earful, but then he kindly asks me if I am ready to board the flight now, and if I would like a hand with those cumbersome carry-ons. I look over my shoulder at all the people glaring at me . . . and then it happened. He said, "It's okay, Ms. Enright, you are in seat 8A, by the window, in our Business Class cabin, is that suitable? You have priority boarding."

I am stunned. Air Canada the airline I love to dislike has upgraded because of the 737 flight change and upgraded my seat. Because of this unexpected airline chaos I am suddenly flying in Business Class for free !!! What are the chances of that? I have my own pod with a lay-flat seat, a desk, a gourmet breakfast, and wine tasting—all starting at 7:39 a.m. EST, and it's only the first day. This is First Class with a capital F!!!

Just so you don't think I am messing with you, I asked my fabulous flight attendant, Donna, to snap a few pics of me enjoying my pod. I am so grateful and so excited; this is definitely a sign things are changing for the better, and it's going to be a super-awesome trip!
Love to all,
Jane

....

Dear Friends and Family,

Greetings from magical Maui!!! So many things to cover I don't know where to start! This update is a little longer than usual. If you can hang in there with me, I promise you an unbelievable ending to my super awesome trip.

When I last left you, I was jetting across the international dateline, well on my way to my redo Wednesday.

When you travel to Oceania, you lose a day; and when you come back, you get to redo that day you lost. This is pure genius on the part of the universe. Personally, I think everyone on the planet should be granted at least one redo day a year; there are a lot of situations where this could come in very handy.

I land in Maui after my fifteen-hour flight from Sydney, grab my luggage, and head down to the tram to take me to the rental car centre. I am all settled in, (by now I'm a professional, this is my tenth international flight in forty-five days), when the conductor announces the tram is broken and everyone needs to start walking. Remember Steve Martin in that movie Planes, Trains and Automobiles? Just imagine 200 Steve Martins hoofing it down the highway.

I finally get to Alamo and head to the parking lot to pick out my mid-size SUV. Except, when I arrive, there is not a car in sight. I say to clipboard guy, "Busy day?". He says, "It was nuts, how about I give you a van?" I ponder this offer for a minute and tell him I'm looking for something a little sportier. He pauses a moment, looks off in the distance, and says; "okay you can have that one over there." That one, gleaming in the distance, is a brand new fully loaded never driven super high-end jeep with every bell and whistle one could ever wish or hope for in a vehicle; especially if one is driving in Maui. I promptly take this as a sign that even though I have just left my children in Australia, am travelling by myself , and recovering from dengue fever, Maui is going to be wonderful and that I am supposed to drive somewhere amazing that would require me to look absolutely fabulous in a fabulous vehicle; destination TBD.

With that, I hop into my ride, turn up the volume on my surround sound stereo, and head down the coast to Wailea and my super awesome hotel, the Fairmont Kea Lani. After a few days by the pool, some beach walks, and a visit to the Willow Stream Spa, I decide its time to start driving again. Not knowing where I should go, I do what every single girl might do; I call my mom. Sheila, (aka my mom), picks up and she is full of good ideas. Like me Sheila loves to travel and has already been to Maui. Bottom line: Sheila says I need to go to Lahaina, which is a very picturesque forty-kilometer drive from my hotel.

I arrive in Lahaina and it is everything Mom said it would be; quaint, kitschy boutiques, gorgeous sea views, and inviting restaurants. It also turns out Lahaina is home to dozens of unique, top notch art galleries with artists you would not find anywhere else. I walk into gallery number five and the guy behind the desk says, "nice hat." I am wearing my lucky hat, and this hat has been my albatross. I bought this hat in Fiji and I have lost this hat numerous times throughout my journey. However, every time I lose it, it has faithfully been returned to me. Boat crews have retrieved it from shark infested Fijian waters, flight attendants have painstakingly kept it intact in overhead cargo bins, and kind strangers have picked it up off seats when I forgot it in airports. And now, if it were not for this hat, I might not have met the guy behind the desk.

A piece in his shop catches my eye and we start talking. I find out back in the day the proprietor, an accomplished entrepreneur, owned several galleries globally. I quickly surmise that not only is he an astute businessman and very knowledgeable art enthusiast, *he is also very charming. He quickly sees my interest in these magnificent artworks and decides I need to go big or go home. Then, he promptly tries to talk me into a $25,000.00 USD stunning metal work by artist Dennis Mattison. He then tries to sweeten the deal by offering to buy me dinner with lots of wine at the best restaurant in Lahaina to celebrate. I tell him that sounds like a pretty expensive date.*

On my way out the door he tells me he is having an art show that evening. "My best guys are coming, why don't you join us." Now you have to appreciate I am skeptical, and of course safety conscious because I am travelling on my own. After some sunset yoga and a lovely follow-up call from him, I decide that he does not fit the FBI profile of an axe murderer and accept his invitation.

What an amazing evening that was; I met genuine people who also happen to be extraordinary artists. One of the highlights was meeting Ruby Mazur, the creator of the Rolling Stones lips and teeth logo. Ruby is seventy-two years old and unstoppable; an inspirational man who overcame polio to become an incredible artist painting the most famous celebrities in the world. The extraordinary thing is that all the artists I met, my host included, never intentionally set out to do what they are doing now; they followed their hearts and their passion, overcame adversity, and with hard work, things fell into place.

Over dinner I asked the artists if I was going to do one thing in Maui what would it be? It was unanimous; everyone said I must do the Road to Hana tour. Like Route 66 in California, the Road to Hana is an iconic white knuckle but worth it drive with lots of twists and turns, narrow lanes, and incredible landscape and scenery. Since it's a 10 1/2–hour drive round trip and I am on my own, they recommended Temptation Tours. Temptation Tours gives you a luxury-van tour one way, and a return trip via helicopter along the Maui Coast. I decided this would be the perfect way to end my trip and secure a spot before I am scheduled to fly home.

My Road to Hana day arrives and it is picture perfect; bright, clear blue skies, a light breeze and abundant sunshine. However, when I check in at the heliport, I find out there has been a delay; the rest of my tour party is stuck in a traffic jam. After about forty minutes Clarice from Temptation calls me again and tells me we're going to have to cancel this trip; the road from Lahaina has been closed. I tell her I'm disappointed, I was really looking forward to this trip—it was the highlight of my visit to Maui. And then it happened . . . amidst crisis Clarice pauses on the other end of the phone and puts me on hold. I'm waiting, and waiting, and finally about ten minutes later she comes back on the line and says, "Ms. Enright, I don't know why this is happening, I've worked here eleven years, and this has never happened before, but you are getting a private tour of Maui today. Your helicopter pilot Gary will be picking you up and together you will fly along the coastline for an hour and see whatever you wish. Then, you'll land at Hana airport where your driver Whitney will be waiting with your gourmet picnic lunch to take you anywhere you want to go. I hope you enjoy Maui."

I am both stunned and speechless; not only at the generosity of the offer, but at the possibilities that lay before me in such a magical place. I have truly never experienced this much abundance in my life, let alone all in one day; and what a spectacular day it was!

I saw waterfalls and jaw dropping coastline in a 4.5-million-dollar helicopter, swam under cascading waterfalls, explored a rainforest and drank in scenery that took my breath away; it was truly eye candy for the soul. All the while, Gary and Whitney couldn't do enough for me; they were my guardian angles who made me feel like a celebrity. Ironically when we stopped for a tour at Waianpanapa State Park I heard a woman say, "I wonder who that is?" Her companion replied, "I don't know, but I think I saw her on Ellen once."

Of course, after a day like this one I couldn't just head back to my hotel and call it a night, I had to celebrate! I suggested to my tour guide Whitney we grab drinks and dinner on me so I could thank her for a great day. I already knew where I wanted to go; I wanted to go to Mama's Fish House. Now you must appreciate Mama's is one of the top restaurants in the USA, and NO ONE gets into Mama's without a reservation. In fact, I started trying to secure a table at Mama's before I even left Australia, no luck. So, I said to Whitney; "I'm going to take a chance, just show up and see what happens . . ."

I hopped in my fabulous jeep and set off for Mama's. When I arrived, their valet asked me if I would be dining with them this evening . . . I replied, "You bet I am!" I walked over to the hostess and started telling her about my day, and said, "You know what would be the cherry on top of this sundae (remember, I'm in marketing), is if I could have dinner at Mama's with my friend Whitney. Do you think you could find any space for us?" The receptionist looked at me, smiled, and said, "Of course we can!" A divine ending to a divine day, which I am certain would not have happened without faith, hope, gratitude, and divine intervention. I am definitely too blessed to be stressed!

Thanks for hanging in there with me. Mahalo and Aloha!

Love Jane

CHAPTER FOURTEEN

Change Can Change
Its Mind Any time

....

In the midst of every crisis lies opportunity.
—ALBERT EINSTEIN

L ife puts us all through unplanned change. However, sometimes the unexpected or unthinkable can occur. The 2020 COVID-19 pandemic is a sound example of this. We knew that another pandemic could happen; however, many of us never thought it would happen. Now, no matter who you are, or where you live, on some level everything seems upside down, not right-side up.

Disasters such as COVID-19 are an accelerator for change. Who knew that at any given moment a package of toilet paper could suddenly become more valuable than your stock portfolio, or that in a heartbeat, face masks and social distancing would become the new global norm? To say the world has experienced, and will continue to experience, unprecedented change for decades would be the understatement of the year. In a nutshell: COVID-19 is unplanned change on steroids.

Unfortunately, rapid unplanned change such as a pandemic also brings with it prolonged uncertainty. When this happens, it is normal to have difficulty seeing the upside of things. We are grieving the way things used to be (loss) and are fearful about what may, or may not, happen in the future (anxiety). Some anxiety is useful because it helps us initiate strategies like social distancing to reduce risk and keep ourselves safe. However, if we let them, sadness, fear, and anxiety can quickly become panic and cast a stranglehold on our ability to cope and move forward through uncertain times. The question then becomes how do we successfully navigate change when change can change its mind anytime?

When disaster strikes, maintaining a positive mindset with faith and hope becomes more important than ever before. Just like we put those cases of water and week's worth of groceries in the pantry, having a positive mindset is emergency preparedness for our minds. Maintaining a positive perspective during prolonged uncertainty can make the difference between having a super-awesome life or a super-rotten one while massive upheaval plays out.

Mastering the art of positive thinking when you don't know what the next five minutes might bring can be challenging. Positive thinking gives us an extreme advantage during times of extreme stress; yet most people do not use this strategy to their advantage. As humans we tend to focus our time and energy on what we don't have, rather than on what we do have. Throw in some catastrophic change and we are naturally waiting for the other shoe to drop like everyone else.

During any type of change, the first step towards successfully moving away from negative thoughts towards more positive ones is acceptance.[23] This does not mean you have to be happy about a situation like a pandemic and negate how it

23. Please refer to the OMG Takeaway section for examples.

disrupted your life—or happy all the time. That is unrealistic. It means that to move forward, not backward, one has to try and accept change is happening, not resist or deny it. Acceptance and looking at your circumstances from the outside in, rather than the inside out, helps take the emotionality (fear, sadness, anxiety) out of situations. Regardless of the magnitude of an event, this encourages our minds to shift to a more positive end of the spectrum.

If we take COVID-19 as an example, the upside is that we are all in this together; friends, colleagues, family, and people around the world can relate and empathize with each other. This pandemic is not just changing your life; it is changing and affecting everyone's lives at the same time. Collectively there is, and will be, coordinated assistance and support such as food banks, medical care, financial programs, and mental-health resources to help populations deal with and navigate this unprecedented change. Friends, businesses, neighborhoods, schools, and communities will adapt to make things better and help each other. Moreover, a pandemic illuminates systemic problems crying out for change, things that need to be changed for the better, such as wiping out racism, supporting our health-care workers, and caring for our most vulnerable populations. Technologically, we will see advances in medical care and the ways we communicate with each other at a distance.

With COVID-19, many people have experienced, or will experience an unforeseen employment interruption such as a layoff or job loss. Some individuals will choose to view this unplanned change as an opportunity to pause, reflect, and re-evaluate their futures. This is where an environmental scan can be useful to look at a situation like unemployment more objectively and identify what we can control and what we cannot control. Consequently, outside-in thinking can empower us to see the big picture, explore options, and discover opportunities amidst crisis.

Taking one day at a time is also key to coping and successfully navigating stressful situations, but particularly ones involving prolonged uncertainty. Mindfulness supports any journey to successfully navigate change because staying in the present reduces anxiety about the future and depression about the past. This helps us calm our thinking and be better prepared to stickhandle unexpected change as it arises. Tools such as meditation, exercise, and creating new, purposeful routines are great strategies to pre-pave our days and set the course for fulfilling outcomes.

Practicing gratitude during times of enormous change is also extremely important. While gratitude does not make you immune to negative feelings, it can make you more resilient because it magnifies positive emotions rather than negative ones.[24] Research has shown practicing gratitude can have a transformative effect on individuals' lives because people with a more grateful disposition are more likely to bounce back after times of great adversity.[25] Individuals who practice gratitude are also more likely to have a proactive coping style, and less likely to develop post-traumatic stress disorder (PTSD). They are also more likely to view challenges as opportunities for personal growth.[26] Keeping a gratitude journal during tough times can help you get into the habit of practicing gratitude daily and being more mindful. Studies show that people who do this feel far less anxious and depressed than people who do not.[27]

Affirmations are another tool that can help us move towards a more confident frame of mind during times of uncertainty. An affirmation is consciously choosing words to bring or not bring something into your life such as, "I am

---

24. Emmons, Robert. *Greater Good Magazine*, University of California at Berkley, November 16, 2010
25. Ibid
26. Ibid
27. Ibid

choosing to think more positively about this situation today." Being grateful for what you do have, instead of focusing on what you don't have, helps us stay positive and can illuminate our path as we navigate troubled times.

Unprecedented change like COVID-19 brings with it hard, tough stuff. The flipside is, as with all unplanned change, no matter what the magnitude, there will be fresh starts. Change can open doors; bring us joy, happiness, and excitement; offer new opportunities and experiences; usher in new love and friendships; and build faith, hope, strength, and courage we never knew we had.

COVID-19 is a reminder to all of us that change can change its mind any time, and that we need to do everything possible and use every resource in the toolkit so we can land butter-side up, not butter-side down in the game of life. Now more than ever, it is important to keep perspective and remember our life is what we create. Positive thoughts have a good effect on us. They can support us to become happier and healthier and add value to our entire lives, especially during times of prolonged uncertainty. By recognizing the impact of negative thoughts on our minds and well-being, we can more easily begin to replace negative thinking with more positive choices.

Stuff with four letters ending in a *T* happens to all of us; it's how you handle it that matters. Our thoughts are just thoughts, and we are free to choose new thoughts and positive thinking any time, especially during challenging, changing times.[28] Maintaining a more positive mindset can help you find silver linings and opportunities amidst downturns, attract more brightness into your life, and successfully stickhandle the unexpected so you can create a new storyline—no matter what the situation.

---

28. Louise Hay. Louisehay.com

Am I going to sugar-coat this and tell you that it is easy to change your habits? No. It takes diligence and support to change things for the better. However, I am a walking, talking infomercial for the unexpected. I have learned first hand that it is possible to reframe your thinking, be mindful, change your mindset, and get positive results.. In the end, it is important to have faith and believe that everything will work out, and that you can successfully navigate change, make your ideas happen, and land butter-side up in the game of life—even during a pandemic. Sometimes you just need some inspiration to believe that what seems impossible, is possible . . . just ask my friend Adesh!

OMG: Stuff with four letters ending in a *T* happens to everyone; it's how you handle it that matters.

—JANE ENRIGHT

All I Really Need to Know
I Learned in Kindergarten
. . . and at the Flower Shop

BY JANE ENRIGHT

Thursday mornings are my favourite. That's because Thursday mornings are reserved for Miss Harrison and her kindergarten class at G.R. Allen School. Today is extra special though; it's my first day, and we are making Father's Day cards. Miss Harrison has set up discovery stations in the classroom, and I am stationed at "the flower shop," cutting out paper ties that we will decorate together.

All my new kindergarten friends are super-excited, and like Curious George, are curious about me with a bazillion questions. "Who are you? Why are you here? Where do you live? I like your shoes. Are you staying for nutrition break? You have grey in your hair. Are you Miss Harrison's mother? Do you have any pets? I have a fish . . . can I help you cut?" Finally, like herding cats, I manage to satisfy their curiosity (or so I think), when a small boy tapped me on the shoulder and says, "Excuse me, is the flower shop open today?"

Now I haven't met this little fellow yet, but I can tell he's all business and very keen to open the flower shop for the day. Technically, according to "the rules," you are not supposed to go to the flower shop, or any other discovery station, until your other work is complete. I know this, not just because Miss Harrison told me so, but because this is not my first rodeo teaching elementary school. When I was in my early twenties, I had a stint teaching kindergarten, grade one, and grade four in a fly-in community called Sachigo Lake, underneath Hudson's Bay. At the time, we had no running water, but we had kindergarten.

I stick out my hand and introduce myself. "Hi, I'm Jane, what's your name?"

Little guy says with a big toothy grin, "I got my journal done. Is the flower shop open yet?"

I quickly surmise this kid is perceptive, and also masterful at redirecting the conversation. I laugh and say, "Of course it is—but who is going to be on cash, you or me?"

It turns out the little guy's name is Adesh, and when I ask him if he comes here often, he replies, "I love the flower shop. I come here nearly every day." After he carefully rings up my bouquet, on the Fisher-Price digital cash register and gives me my change, I said to him, "You know, Adesh, you really seem to like it here; perhaps you could own your own flower shop someday?"

For a moment I could see his mind and imagination wander, and then the light bulb went on. I witnessed first hand Adesh experiencing the power of imagining and believing that, yes, he too could own his own flower shop someday. Watching him took me back in time to my own childhood. It reminded me that to follow our life's purpose, and overcome obstacles, all we really need to do is remember those lessons we learned in kindergarten—including the power to believe in yourself and be playful, and if you can dream it, you can do it!

Later, as we were closing the flower shop together for the day, Adesh turned to me and asked, "When were you born?"

Smart kid. He wanted to know if I was legit.

When I told him the year, he turned to me, mouth gaping and exclaimed, "YOU ARE SOOO OLD!"

OMG:
This
Believing
Stuff . . .
It Really
Works!

CHAPTER FIFTEEN

My Crystal Ball
is in The Shop

....

*"Believe In Yourself And The Universe
Is Forced To Believe In You*

—VIC JOHNSON

"Hi Jane, its Christopher. I'm just calling you to see if you sent me your stuff yet?"

It is a sunny Saturday afternoon in the middle of February 2020. I am having lunch in Nate's backyard (the demo guy), in beautiful Beaver Valley. Long story short: Nate is my friend Joanne's nephew who has a beautiful cabin beside the Beaver River. Her sister Brenda is his mother. Along with our friend Linda, and my friend Patty, we have become ski sisters. I am celebrating, because after 43 years I have returned to Beaver Valley Ski Club (BVSC) as a member,

"Sorry Christopher, I haven't had time, I'm skiing today."

I'm back here largely because I volunteered to help with the BVSC Memorial Forest Project. Early in 2019, I learned there was a memoriam being installed to honour former members who, like my friend Jenn, and her father, had passed away. I made a donation to their fundraising gala to support the effort, and worked with members this past summer to plan the project. In the midst of it, all the general manager offered me a super awesome deal on a ski membership that I couldn't refuse. Returning to BVSC has been a joyful addition to my life. It is a great way to give back to the community, honour Jenn's memory, and a wonderful opportunity to create new memories with friends that bring me happiness and fun!

"Jane I looked at your website, and was impressed. Are you going to send me your stuff?"

The website Christopher is referring to is mysuper awesomelife.com. I created MSAL in September 2019 to share inspirational stories and know-how to help people like me, cope with unexpected change. This time "my stuff" does not have four letters ending in a T. It is four sample book chapters that I have meticulously been writing and rewriting since my impromptu date with the publisher. Not quite knowing whether he was buttering me up, or being totally sincere, I decided I needed a second opinion. So in October 2019 I contacted an editor, (Jaclyn from Nest and Story), and asked her to give me an honest opinion about whether I could take this story anywhere. Her answer was a resounding yes!

After that conversation I worked with Jaclyn off and on to edit and refine my sample chapters. Jaclyn helped me "learn the biz" and gave me the encouragement I needed to successfully navigate the publishing world. The first piece of advice I received from Jaclyn was that if you are going to author a book you need to be comfortable with the word "no"—there is a lot of rejection and judgement in this field. She also helped me complete an environmental scan (SWOT), to shortlist publishers and pinpoint who might be most receptive to new authors. Finally, in January 2020 she said "Jane, you're ready!" With that I prayed to the publishing fairies to smile kindly on me.

My first query letter went to Page Two Books in Vancouver. Their process started with asking me to describe in 200 words or less who I was, what my book was about, and why I wanted to work with them. Thankfully I passed that test, and was a sign for me there was light at the end of the tunnel. I then went on to stage two and sent them my sample chapters. I heard back two weeks later from their senior editor Amanda with the nicest no ever. Amanda said that she loved my writing, but was concerned that my outline might not be comprehensive enough. In other words, similar to what Matt "the kid" had said to Clayton about rehab, in her opinion, I was "not a good candidate at this time."

After receiving Amanda's advice, I sketched out my chapter takeaways and formalized my chapter messages. I did so to ensure I would not miss anything I felt was important. Otherwise, I may never have found a publisher! Out of something negative, came something very positive. Amanda gave me some wonderful feedback, which not only encouraged me to do my best, but confirmed I was headed in the right direction with my butter-side up theory. Outside-in thinking enabled me to remain focused on the big picture and not get caught in the weeds of feeling rejected.

"Thanks for calling Christopher. I wasn't sure I was ever going to hear from you again."

Christopher is the editor I had a conversation with after Amanda. He picked up the phone on a snowy day in February and said flat out that he was very reluctant to take on an unfinished manuscript. I told him during our call that because I was a new writer, I felt I needed support along the way from a strong editor—that it made absolutely no business sense for me to complete a manuscript to be told afterwards that it was not what the publisher wanted.

After listening to a bit more to my story he asked, "How long do you think it will take you to finish writing the book?"

To which I replied, "I don't know. My crystal ball is in the shop and quite honestly, I've never written a book."

That's when he said, " Jane, I'm late for my meeting. I should have been there thirty minutes ago so I need to hang up now."

Quite frankly, after our exchange, I thought I was toast.

It was at that moment, standing in three feet of snow in the middle of Nate the demo guy's backyard in Beaver Valley that Christopher and I reached a compromise. I agreed to send him my chapters, aka "my stuff," and he agreed he would review them and tell me what he thought. He did not promise anything else except that he would make a sincere effort to get back to me within three weeks. Considering the circumstances, I thought this was fair.

The next day a miracle happened. Less than twenty-four hours after receiving "my stuff" Christopher telephoned me and said, "Jane, remember when I told you I was really worried you had not finished your manuscript? Well, I just read your sample chapters and I'm not worried anymore. May I have your email so I can send you a contract?"

To say I was on cloud nine after that phone call would be the understatement of the year. I had visualized this outcome everyday for months since my Sicilian miracle, hoping and praying I would get a positive response from a publisher. I had a great desire to share my knowledge about navigating change with others. I had spent years dealing with the after effects of my concussion, and spent over a hundred consecutive days in Ontario hospitals helping people I loved. Along the way, I experienced and witnessed a lot of traumatic and dramatic change. Although my journey was extremely difficult at times, I knew had skills and know-how others did not that helped me survive, and begin to thrive again. Afterwards, I encountered many people who told me they couldn't believe I had landed butter-side up after what I had been through; they wanted to know "my secret to getting through everything." After some noodling and listening to my intuition, I decided to share my story. I felt a push to share my know-how with others so they could land butter-side up too.

I've always been a go-big-or-go home kind of gal who believes if you don't try, you don't know. I had given myself a year to find a publisher and finish my book. I figured if I did not take the opportunity to see where my writing could take me, I would regret it for the rest of my life. Since I was sidelined from facilitating, I also wanted to take a lemon of a year and try and make cents of it all too with a brand-new career change.

With that, writing *Butter Side Up* became analogous to pregnancy and carrying a child; it was a mindful project that I lovingly carried with me everywhere I went. I wrote chapters in my head when I was walking, driving, cooking dinner, and waking up in the morning. Anytime an idea popped into my head, I would write it down or note it on my cell phone. On the upside, the onset of COVID was a bit of a gift for me because with lockdowns there was nowhere to go and not much to do. Because I felt compelled to write I wrote everywhere and pretty much every day. Like carrying a full-term baby; I started writing *Butter Side Up* in October 2019 and finished it in June 2020—nine months later. I went from writing a few emails to a short story, to publishing a book in a just a year. A miracle for a girl with a head injury who never dreamed of being an author until I was forced to rethink my life when the unthinkable happened—three times over!

For me, *Butter Side Up* is not a therapeutic journey; it is a gateway to starting a brand a new chapter, literally and figuratively, in my life. I know there are about a million people in the world that would love to have this opportunity to share their thoughts and make a difference. I take writing seriously and am mindful that like our thoughts, our words are powerful things. I am very grateful for the opportunity to have a new career that I love, collaborate with like-minded individuals, and help others.

Right now, like many of us, my crystal ball is still in the shop and I don't know what the next five minutes might bring. If someone had told me four years ago I would be writing the second edition of a book on unplanned change during a pandemic I would have told them I don't believe them. However now I know better. I also know that hard work pays off. I am blessed to have a new publisher She Writes Press and be collaborating with a talented, thoughtful group of authors who support me and my work which I am so very grateful for.

Even during uncertain times, I still believe there is hope on the horizon. I have faith that with a more optimistic, positive mindset, things in my life have, and will continue, to change for the better. Is everything perfect with my life circumstances? The short answer is no-there is no such thing as a stress free life. There will always be *"stuff,"* good and not so good, in our lives. Ditto for me too. Is my life super awesome? Yes! I have had opportunities, possibilities, and wonderful experiences galore as a result of unexpected curveballs thrown my way out of left field. When I started to believe things could be different, and said "I am tired of hard and sad, and want things to be the opposite of that"—that's when my life started to change for the better.

How we choose to respond to change can make the difference between staying stuck with our challenges, or utilizing these life changing experiences as opportunities for growth. I chose the latter, rather than the former. I chose to try and have a super awesome life—no matter what. I am honoured and grateful to have the opportunity to share my thoughts, ideas, and know-how with you. I hope sharing my story has inspired you to have hope that things can change for the better in your life too. In that spirit, I have included strategies in my OMG Resources section and on my website, mysuperawesomelife.com, to help you look on the bright side and support you during the days, weeks, months, and years to come to successfully navigate change, create your new storylines, and land butter-side up in the game of life. Believing is believing in yourself, and that you can do anything despite your circumstances. Remember, I believe in you. The question is, do you believe in yourself?

> Believing is having faith in yourself that despite your circumstances, you can do anything. Believing is believing in miracles.
>
> —JANE ENRIGHT

CHAPTER SIXTEEN

The Supporting Actress

....

"Love changes, but it never ends."
—KAREN MCKNIGHT

"Hi J, it's me. I'm just calling to let you know that I made a reservation for lunch next Wednesday. I can't remember the name of the place; it's that Italian restaurant, the one with the table you like by the window."

"Oh wow, that sounds fabulous C—I love that place."

Like most couples, when you uncouple, you need time and space to adapt and adjust to your new roles. After my bon voyage letter to C, subsequent conversations with him about my desire to be in his life, and necessity to do so in a different way—as a supporting actress, rather than a lead one, we had a time out. This included almost seven months with no contact at all. Those months were challenging, confusing, and painful—for both of us. At times I wondered if I would ever have any contact with Clayton again. Then one day, out of the blue, a miracle happened. C wrote me an email that said:

Hi Jane,
*   Just wondering if you were still interested in get-*
ting together for a conversation/chat.
Sincerely,
Clayton

Since that e-mail, C and I have worked hard to create a new and improved storyline; a fresh start with a clean slate. This includes meeting for lunch or dinner often. It not only gives us the opportunity to keep in touch, it gives us time together to support and encourage one another, create new memories, and reminisce about happy moments. "J, I'm hoping you might be able to join me for lunch. I have something important to ask you."

I smile. "C, you are always so thoughtful. I know what you are going to ask me, and I would love to join you for lunch."

He chuckles. "Well, you know, J, just because we didn't get married doesn't mean I can't keep asking."

"Of course it doesn't. Besides, if you didn't remember to keep asking me, I might think something was wrong, like maybe you'd fallen and hit your head again."

We both laugh out loud.

"Me too, J. Me too!"

Clayton and I both continue to live very separate lives, but we also continue to look out for each other. For instance, during the pandemic lockdown which lasted for months I often found groceries I never ordered on my porch, and C often found dinners he never made on his doorstep. The two of us want the very best for each other; and no one is more supportive of my writing than C. In fact, I still receive flowers almost every week, delivered anonymously, from "your greatest fan." Clayton is back to writing and teaching a bit too. We still love and care for each other, but in a different way. I am a supporting actress in C's life now, rather than the lead one. Sometimes though, it is difficult for others to understand our relationship in this context. People often believe when you break up, it has to be all or nothing. Yet, it is the exact opposite for us. Because of our circumstances, we needed to change. We chose to see things for what they are, rather than what they could have been. An ending brought us a new beginning with a joyful new chapter that both C and I continue to be very grateful for. Love changes, but it never ends.

> When you're finished changing, you're finished.
> —BENJAMIN FRANKLIN

OMG:
Resources
for
Everyday
Living

Why OMG Is Key to Landing Butter Side Up

We all have moments in our lives when the unexpected happens—a sudden change in circumstances that takes us by surprise. Sometimes these moments bring us joy and happiness. Other times, they feel devastating and make us ask "Why me?" When the latter happens, it is easy to get stuck in a loop of anger, sadness, resentment, and denial. But when we find ourselves reeling from unexpected change, it is helpful to remember that we can choose to accept that change has happened and to move forward in a positive way.

ACCEPTANCE

Acceptance is the first step towards successfully navigating change.

Acceptance is the first step towards navigating change of any kind—but especially rapid, unexpected change. Accepting a new reality does not mean that you have to like or be happy about what is happening. It simply means that you don't resist, reject, or deny your new circumstances. If you accept that rapid unexpected change, good or bad, can happen at any time, you set the stage for using strategies such as Outside-in Thinking, Mindfulness, and Gratitude more effectively.

Acceptance Benefits

Acceptance helps you move forward, shift your perspective, and develop a more positive mindset. Acceptance can also help you become a more flexible thinker and foster your ability to respond to changes productively rather than react to them impulsively.

Try This

Affirmations are a powerful tool for successfully navigating change. They are statements that help you focus on what you *can* do, rather than what you *can't* do. When you repeat affirmations, you talk to yourself about what you want to bring, or not bring, into your life. Author Louise Hay dedicated her life to helping us understand affirmations and that the thoughts we think and the words we speak are constantly shaping our world and our future. Our thoughts are just thoughts, and we don't have to be held captive to the emotions our thoughts create.

Affirmations for Acceptance[29]

1. I accept there are no mistakes in life, just lessons.
2. I accept others as they are, without trying to change them.
3. I accept that I am free to choose positive thoughts and new ways of thinking any time.
4. I accept responsibility for my life and creating my own happiness.

---

29. Louisehay.com

5. I enthusiastically accept love, joy, and happiness into my life in abundance.
6. I accept what is with a peaceful mind.
7. I lovingly accept that I am enough.

OUTSIDE-IN THINKING

**Outside-in thinking helps you
visualize and plan the route.**

Outside-in thinking, or big picture thinking, is looking at your life as an observer rather than as a participant. In other words, being in the audience rather than in the play and "watching" your feelings and behavior unfold as a situation is happening.

Outside-in Thinking Benefits

Manageable Feelings

Outside-in thinking helps us cope with emotions such as fear and sadness, which are stored in the parts of our brain called the amygdala and hypothalamus.[30] These areas of the brain also trigger the fight, flight, and freeze responses to things we perceive as threatening, which is what unwanted change often feels like. But these are impulsive responses to *physical* threats. Most of the time, the threats posed by unwanted changes are psychological. It's just that our brain needs help seeing the difference. This is where outside-in thinking comes in: It helps us distinguish between actual and perceived threats, which can take the power out of emotions that get in the way of clear thinking.

30. brainfacts.org/thinking-sensing-and-behaving/emotions-stress-and-anxiety/2018/

Productive Thinking

Observing yourself—your behaviour and patterns, as well as what makes you happy and unhappy—from the outside in can help you set intentions that align with positive activities and routines. Doing this will reinforce your new mindset and goals. Your thoughts help you visualize and create a plan for what comes next, which promotes and reinforces acceptance, reduces fear, and helps you find the upside when you need it.

Increased Creativity

Looking at yourself from outside in also can help you be a more creative thinker. It helps you focus on your strengths, recognize but not judge yourself for your weaknesses, mitigate risk, and improve objectivity. It also sharpens your decision-making so that you can take advantage of opportunities and avenues you may not have thought of before. In doing so, you will be better equipped to be more solution-driven, purposeful, and adaptable after unplanned change.

Try This

Pretend you are in the audience at a play about the story of your life. Take a scan of the scene you're in now. Think of something you want to change for the better and then visualize the end goal first: a scene in your life that you would like to watch a year from now, one with a happy ending or maybe one that you would like to wrap up so that you can start fresh. Whether you are recovering from an illness, focusing on personal development, or navigating a crisis, identifying your end goal makes it easier to see routines, priorities, and areas of focus that need to change now so that you can make the plotline you visualize a reality.

MINDFULNESS

Mindfulness supports you
as you navigate the journey.

A good speaker knows the importance of pauses between words. A talented musician understands that silence between notes is as much a part of the symphony as the music itself. Similarly, taking things one day at a time, staying present, and being mindful is key to successfully navigating stressful situations, particularly ones involving prolonged uncertainty. Mindfulness supports you as you navigate change because staying in the present helps you pause, calm your thoughts, and reduce the need to focus on events of the past or the future.

Mindfulness Benefits

Improved Brain Function

Mindfulness helps you focus your thoughts and emotions on the present. By relaxing your body and your brain you are clearing the clutter from your mind so that your thought processes and decision-making are clearer.

Stress Relief and Joy

Meditation, or "purposeful mindfulness," reduces cortisol—a hormone related to stress.[31] When we're meditating, we're focused on the present and not as likely to think and worry about what will happen or won't happen.

---

31. https://www.health.harvard.edu/blog/mindfulness-meditation-helps-fight-insomnia-improves-sleep-201502187726

Improved Sleep and Productivity

Have you ever gone to bed worrying about something? The good news is that mindfulness meditation exercises work even after your head hits the pillow. Research has shown that mind-calming practices can reduce sleep disturbances by releasing melatonin in our brains that helps regulate our sleep patterns.[32]

Try This

Find a mobile app, website, or class that guides you through meditations or a yoga practice. Exercise and establishing purposeful routines are also great strategies for practicing mindfulness and setting the course for fulfilling outcomes. These activities can calm and clarify our thinking and help us set our compass for the day so we can manage our emotional health no matter what happens.

GRATITUDE

Gratitude illuminates the path.

Gratitude is an affirmation of goodness, and it's an underused tool that helps us respond to change, especially the unpleasant kind. Recognizing what you have to be grateful for after an unplanned, unwanted change can be challenging, though. It's human nature to spend time and energy mourning what we have lost and forget to appreciate what we have. Throw in the prolonged uncertainty that comes with some disruptions—like a global pandemic—and feelings of depression, anxiety,

32. Ibid

and sadness over our losses can multiply exponentially. The antidote is to acknowledge things, even small things, that you have to be thankful for. While we cannot control what happens during times of prolonged uncertainty, we can control our reaction to it. Recognize that despite life's challenges, you can manage how your day will unfold. Our intention creates our reality, and gratitude illuminates the path by helping us focus on our blessings and stay positive.

Gratitude Benefits

Resiliency

While gratitude does not make you immune to negative feelings, it can make you more resilient, because it magnifies positive emotions rather than negative ones. Research has shown that people with a more grateful disposition are more likely to bounce back after great adversity.[33] Individuals who practice gratitude are more likely to have a pro-active coping style and seek out social support in times of need. They are also less likely to develop post-traumatic stress disorder and are more likely to see opportunities for growth in times of stress.[34]

Improved Well Being

When you acknowledge that you have worthwhile things in your life, it's like you're reminding yourself that you're *worthy*, too. Having an increased sense of self-worth is a huge key to mental and physical well-being.[35]

33. greatergood.berkeley.edu/article/item/why_gratitude_is_good Robert Emmons, November 16, 2010
34. Ibid
35. Ibid

Positive Perspective

American monk David Steindl-Rast said, "It is not happiness that makes us grateful, but gratefulness that makes us happy." Gratitude helps us feel more positive emotions, relish good experiences, deal with adversity, and build strong relationships. Moving forward after unplanned change is much easier with a positive mindset.

Try This

Make a list of simple gratitude statements that you can repeat to yourself when you observe yourself focusing on the negative. Self-talk such as "I am still breathing today," "I have food to eat," and "I am healthy" can recalibrate your mind when change has thrown you off balance. You could also start keeping a gratitude journal, listing things you are grateful for daily. This will help you get into the habit of practicing gratitude and being more mindful. Studies show that people who do this feel far less anxious and depressed than people who do not.

Outside-in thinking helps you
visualize and plan the route.

Mindfulness supports the journey.

Gratitude illuminates the path.

Outside-in thinking. Mindfulness. Gratitude™

Suggestions for
Further Reading

Here are some suggestions for further reading to help you successfully navigate change, make your ideas happen, and create your new storylines.

Aronson, Brad. *HumanKind: Changing the World One Small Act At a Time.* **LifeTree Media, 2020.**
I discovered this title, and author Brad Aronson, (now a treasured colleague), while researching publishing opportunities. Brad's life changed when his wife Mia was diagnosed with leukemia. Inspired by the generosity of spirit, he began writing about the people who rescued his family from that dark time, often with the smallest of gestures. *HumanKind* will leave you grateful for what you have. This book is also a reminder of what really matters and how you can change a life—including your own!

Bridges, William. *Transitions: Making Sense of Life's Changes.* **Da Capo Press, 2004.**
In the 1970s, William Bridges started the conversation about making sense of life's changes and strategies to cope with them. This is a worthwhile read for anyone trying to decipher

the psychology behind the various stages of one's life and what comes next.

Burnett, Bill and Evans, Dave. *Designing Your Life: How to Build a Well-Lived, Joyful Life.* **Knopf Doubleday Publishing, 2016.**
Designing Your Life is about taking control of your life; creating a plan that will do away with the traditional nine-to-five routine and usher in a career that you really love. You will find advice and exercises that will point you toward your true calling, along with progressive ideas that challenge the limitations of traditional career counselling.

Carnine, Doug. *How Love Wins: The Power of Mindful Kindness.* **Mindful Kindness Project, 2017.**
In this simple but powerful guide, Professor Doug Carnine leads the reader through a twelve-step process of transformation, opening a toolbox of skills and techniques that anyone can use to live more fully in the moment and be more kind to themselves and others. Carnine reassures us that everyone is capable of building a mindfully kind life—and making it stick.

Chilton, David. *The Wealthy Barber: Everyone's Common-Sense Guide to Becoming Financially Independent.* **Stoddart Publishing Ltd., 1989.**
Considered to be a cornerstone of financial planning, *The Wealthy Barber* gives practical, common-sense advice and strategies about how to manage your finances successfully to help you live your best life.

Coloroso, Barbara. *Kids Are Worth It: Giving Your Child the Gift of Inner Discipline.* **Somerville House Publishing, 1995.**
If you believe kids are worth it, then you need to read this book. An inspiring guide to help you find your parenting style

and help your child make good decisions that will carry them through a lifetime.

Dyer, Wayne. *Change Your Thoughts, Change Your Life: Living the Wisdom of the Tao.* **Hay House Inc., 2007.**
An inspirational thoughtful book about how the power of thought can change your life.

Enright, Jane. mysuperaweomelife.com. 2019.
For me My Super-Awesome Life™ is all about trying to be more optimistic, looking for the positive during our struggles, and living your best life. MSAL is a companion to *Butter Side Up*. It offers weekly inspiration, a monthly newsletter, articles, ideas, and know-how, and support to help you successfully navigate change and look on the bright side so you can create your new storyline and land butter-side up in the game of life.

Foran, Carolyn. *Owning It: Make Your Anxiety Work for You.* **Hachette Ireland, 2017.**
Like me, author Caroline Foran believes in calling a spade a shovel and taking responsibility for your life when things are upside down, not right-side up. Caroline began experiencing crippling anxiety in her early 20s. In *Owning It*, Caroline chronicles her journey from the kind of all-consuming fear where leaving the house for milk was too petrifying a prospect, and holding down a high-octane editor job was no longer possible, to wondering how the hell she was going to pull herself through. But then she did; she owned it!

Fulghum, Robert. *All I Really Need To Know I Learned in Kindergarten: Uncommon Thoughts on Common Things.* **Random House Inc., 1988.**
An inspiring, classic, playful read that is filled with timeless life lessons that are valuable at any age.

Hay, Louise. *You Can Heal Your Life.* Hay House Inc., 2017. Affirmations are a powerful way to plant positive seeds of intention that enable us to refocus our life after trauma and drama. Author Louise Hay explores how patterns of thought create our world and provides know-how and examples to support you to heal your life.

Levin, Jordanna. *Make It Happen: Manifest the Life of your Dreams.* Murdoch Books, Sydney, Australia, 2019.
The word "manifestation" makes most people cringe, including me. Whether you call it visualization, manifestation, or the law of attraction, all these terms essentially mean the same thing; using the power of positive thinking and believing to make your ideas happen. This witty book kept my attention throughout a nineteen-hour flight from Sydney, Australia. It has some great practical tips and real-life scenarios about initiating change; plus, it's a fun read!

Ruiz, Don Miguel. *The Four Agreements: A Practical Guide to Personal Freedom.* Amber Allen Publishing, 1997.
A *New York Times* best seller for over a decade, *The Four Agreements* offers a code of conduct based on ancient Toltec wisdom, which advocates freedom from self-limiting beliefs that may cause suffering and limitations in a person's life.

Singer, Michael A. The *Untethered Soul: The Journey Beyond Yourself.* New Harbinger Publications Inc. and Noetic Books, Oakland, California, 2007.
Michael Singer takes thinking about yourself and your thoughts to a whole new level. *The Untethered Soul* challenges and opens up your mind to new ways of thinking, landing you butter-side up at the end of the journey.

Winfrey, Oprah. *The Path Made Clear: Discovering Your Life's Direction and Purpose.* Melcher Media, 2019
Oprah Winfrey believes every one of us is born with a purpose. *The Path Made Clear* compiles anecdotes and ideas to inspire your personal journey to find, understand, and pursue your life's true calling.

Book Club

Discussion Questions

....

1. What was your initial reaction to *Butter Side Up*? Why did you choose to read it?
2. Was there anything about the book that surprised you?
3. How did you feel reading the book?
4. What aspects of the author's story could you relate to the most?
5. How honest do you think the author was being when she told her story?
6. Did you find the plot predictable? Were you surprised by any twists and turns?
7. What did you think about the structure of *Butter Side Up*? Why do you think the author chose to tell her story this way?
8. Share a favourite quote or passage from *Butter Side Up*. Why did this quote or passage stand out and why was it meaningful to you?
9. Did *Butter Side Up* make you reflect on how you would deal with sudden, unplanned change? If so, what did you learn and how will you apply what you learned in your everyday life?

10. Were there any sections of the book that you identified more with than others? Was there any advice or part of the book that resonated with you?
11. Were there any sections of the book where you doubted the author's advice?
12. If you had the chance to ask the author one question, what would it be?
13. Was the ending satisfying? Is the ending what you expected?
14. Did the book change your opinion or perspective about change?
15. If you were making a movie of *Butter Side Up*, who would you cast and in what roles?

Acknowledgments

If someone asked me what the most challenging part of this book was, my answer would probably be this acknowledgements page. That's because there have been so many people who supported me not only throughout my most terrible year, but afterwards to create my super-awesome life. In fact, I would probably need to write a sequel just to thank everyone. Given that, I am choosing to focus on acknowledging individuals who knowingly, or unknowingly, directly assisted me to write the book. This includes shout outs to the Kimberley General Store and Justin's Oven who kept me nourished with the best tuna sandwiches on the planet while I wrote at the Mary Tyler Moore Cottage.

In terms of people who supported me to write *Butter Side Up* I need to start with my speech pathologist Deidre. Dee helped me develop strategies to overcome deficits from my head injury, including focusing on writing when I could not speak. Her guidance helped me better understand brain injuries so that I could not only help myself, but write about them. She also unwittingly helped me develop a career path that I love and the means to write this book—thanks Dee!

Next up, I would like to thank staff and members at the Beaver Valley Ski Club in Markdale, Ontario. An invitation to write a short memoriam about Jenn for the BVSC newsletter in 2019 morphed from a four-line remembrance into a chronicle about our friendship. There were so many wonderful memories to share I just couldn't stop writing! That story and their kind feedback inspired me to keep writing and became the basis for celebrating my friendship with Jenn in *Butter Side Up*.

I would also like to acknowledge and give a sincere thank you to my friend Kate. Kate or "Miss H", as she is known to her students, was my project coordinator off and on for ten years when I was a strategic planner. Kate returned during the summer of 2019 to help me start My Super-Awesome Life™. Without her assistance and support, I would not have been able to keep focused, find my first publisher, and complete the first edition of *Butter Side Up* in nine months. Kate has been the most super-awesome colleague ever, and a super-awesome friend too.

Tons of love and gratitude to my sons, Ross and Ryan Enright, for their unwavering support, believing in me, and inviting me to "drop them off" in Australia. Ross gave me the gift of time; he stepped in and oversaw business operations so I could concentrate on writing. Moreover, he launched My Super Awesome Life™ into the exciting world of podcasting—a storyline which I hope we will continue to collaborate on for years to come. My son Ryan, a photographer, stepped up to the plate as my creative consultant, helping me review cover designs and layouts for the first edition. He also shared some fabulous writing tips and had the patience of Job while I shared ideas daily at the dinner table.

Special thanks to my talented and insightful editor Heather Martin from Martin Ink and to all the staff at She Writes Press who, like me, are in it to win it and took me to the finish line with this second edition of *Butter Side Up*. Praise to publisher Brooke Warner for her outstanding leadership and commitment to excellence in publishing. Also, a warm shout-out to associate publisher Lauren and editor Krissa for keeping me on track, and pulling things together so we could successfully launch this second edition in spring 2022. Gratitude to my fellow She Writes Press authors who have welcomed me warmly. I am blessed and honoured to be collaborating with this thoughtful group of creators! Kudos to Crystal and her team at Spark Point Studios, as well as Ben at Cameron PM in the UK for enthusiastically introducing *Butter Side Up*, and me, to the world!

Finally, sincere and heartfelt gratitude to Karen McKnight for being my guardian angel and helping me make sense of it all. Karen, you helped me keep my faith and believe in miracles. It is for all this and more that I am truly grateful.

About the Author

J ane Enright is an ordinary person who has survived some extraordinary things. An inspiring and humorous thought leader, author, and speaker, Canadian-based Jane is a former kindergarten teacher, strategic planner, and university lecturer, as well as the founder of My Super Awesome Life Inc. She speaks to audiences seeking answers to overcome a fear of the unknown, grief, stress, loss, depression, anxiety, stagnation, indecision, sadness, and more. From top executives to stay-at-home moms, she is helping audiences throughout North America land "butter side up" and find joy after unplanned change. You can find Jane on LinkedIn and Instagram; for more information, visit her at www.mysuperawesomelife.com or www.janeenrightauthor.com.

Author photo © Ryan Enright/Ryan Enright Photography

Meet the Author

....

What inspired you to write *Butter Side Up*?
Many things really. As I said in Chapter 13, "Making Sense of It All," I believe everything happens for a reason, and for me, along the way, there were many hints of encouragement to write a book that I could not ignore. These hints, particularly my encounter in Sicily, Italy, inspired me tremendously. Moreover, while I initially started to write email updates as a way to communicate events, I sensed there was another reason I was doing this—I just did not know what it was at the time.

There was also a great desire to share my knowledge about navigating change with others. I have spent years dealing with the aftereffects of my own traumatic brain injury (TBI), and spent over a hundred consecutive days in Ontario hospitals helping people I loved. Along the way, I experienced and witnessed a lot of traumatic and dramatic change. Although my journey was very challenging, I had skills and know-how others did not that helped me successfully navigate change.

Afterwards, I encountered many people who told me they couldn't believe I had landed butter-side up after what I had been through; they wanted to know "my secret to getting through everything." After some noodling and listening to my intuition, I decided to share my story. I felt a push to share my know-how with others so they could land butter-side up too.

This is a very personal memoir with many traumatic and sad events. What were the hardest chapters to write and why?
Because this was my first book, starting the book was really the hardest part. Because *Butter Side Up* is a true story, I knew that in order to tell my story I would have to relive everything in some way, shape, or form as I was writing it. When I sat down to write the first chapter, I cried for a good forty-five minutes, and then I just wrote. Chapters ten to twelve were more difficult because, of course, I was reliving letting go of two people I loved: losing a fiancé and partner without a death, and losing my best friend suddenly and tragically. I still get emotional sometimes when I read the chapters about Jenn, not because I am sad, but because we made such lovely memories together, and I understand how special that was. For me, this book was a major step towards beginning a new chapter. A super-awesome way to launch a brand-new start.

What experiences helped shape your ability to write *Butter Side Up*?
Everything! I believe in being as clear and concise as possible when you write, and my experience with teaching kindergarten helped me to learn how to provide information in bite-size pieces. My consulting experience helped me understand how to navigate change from a business perspective and enabled me to transfer those skills. My own experience with a head injury not only helped me empathize and understand C's journey, it helped me understand the feelings and symptoms that go with it. Finally, my role as a caregiver gave me the ability to see the challenges one faces from an advocacy role.

What is your writing strategy and what would you recommend to others beginning a new writing career?

Many authors and writing courses will tell you the first step to effective writing, whether it be a paragraph, essay, story, or book, is having an outline. However, as I said in chapter fifteen, with my head injury I find that difficult to do. For *Butter Side Up*, I drew on my friends and family emails to help me remember events chronologically and accurately so I could organize them accordingly, but I did not have a formal outline as such. I did, however, sketch out my chapter take-aways for my query to publishers, Nonetheless, it wasn't until chapter nine that I actually formalized my outline. I did so to ensure I would not miss anything I felt was important in tying up chapters.

I do believe in writing often and having dedicated time for writing. I usually set a small goal each day, such as "I am going to refine chapter three today." If I get stuck, I take a walk or daydream a little—sometimes I find just going to the kitchen and making a cup of tea helps a concept or idea that was stuck suddenly emerge. Thankfully while I was writing the first edition of *Butter Side Up*, my "supervisor" Buddy was never too far away for consultation; he was a terrific listener.

Another strategy that I try to use, no matter what I am writing, is to look at my work from the outside in, not the inside out—from the viewpoint of the reader. To do that I literally read aloud, not just in my head, everything I write. I even record myself reading paragraphs sometimes so I can envision what it would be like for a reader to be reading my work. It takes time to meticulously go through your work, but if you are truly a writer, and in it to win it, then it is not work to do this; you will do whatever it takes to make your creations the very best that they can be.

Finally, I would also recommend that before you send your query letters and manuscript to publishers, choose your path wisely and do your homework. Ask yourself, "Am I writing to say I wrote a book, or am I writing to establish or enhance an already existing career?" If it is the former, any publisher will do. However, if it is the latter, you need to research and short list publishers that align with your goals and objectives—otherwise you can waste precious time sending your work to people who may never read or appreciate it. I chose the collaborative publishing route because I wanted to maintain the rights to my own work and have an active say in the process. In the end, you have to look at your goals and objectives and align yourself with a publishing partner that complements your values and desired outcomes.

How did you come up with the OMG™ acronym?
That took a bit of thinking. My experiences taught me that when you are navigating a crisis you don't have time to read a textbook about how to do it. I wanted to share my concepts in a fun way that was easy to understand and remember, so after some days of doodling and noodling, I came up with OMG™.

When you are not writing, what do you like to do?
I do love to write; however, I believe in living a balanced life too. I am a very active person with many interests—spending time with my family and friends is important to me. When I'm not writing, I love to travel, entertain or be outdoors cycling, walking or hiking, golfing, practicing yoga, or in the winter, at the top of Beaver Valley Ski Club, waiting for another run. Race ya!

Next Up from Jane Enright: *Jane's Jam*: A Playbook to *Butter Side Up*

J*ane's Jam* is your playbook for putting the concepts in *Butter Side Up* into action in your life. Packed with practical strategies for increasing outside-in thinking, mindfulness, and gratitude, *Jane's Jam* teaches you how to think and respond more positively to unwanted change. It's full of tools and inspiration that will help you find contentment and joy in any circumstance, letting you taste sweetness even when life goes sour.

You have the power to create your own reality. In *Jane's Jam*, you will learn how to tap into that power and make choices that will lead you to the super-awesome life you deserve.

 My Super **Awesome** Life ™

https://www.janeenrightauthor.com
https://shewritespress.com

janeenright.author

Butter Side Up with Author Jane Enright

@JaneEnright_Author

Jane Enright

SELECTED TITLES FROM SHE WRITES PRESS

She Writes Press is an independent publishing
company founded to serve women writers everywhere.
Visit us at www.shewritespress.com.

Painting Life: My Creative Journey Through Trauma by Carol K.
Walsh. $16.95, 978-1-63152-099-0. Carol Walsh was a psycho-
therapist working with traumatized clients when she encountered
her own traumatic experience; this is the story of how she used
creativity and artistic expression to heal, recreate her life, and
ultimately thrive.

*The Thriver's Edge: Seven Keys to Transform the Way You Live,
Love, and Lead* by Donna Stoneham. $16.95, 978-1-63152-980-1.
A "coach in a book" from master executive coach and leadership
expert Dr. Donna Stoneham, *The Thriver's Edge* outlines a
practical road map to breaking free of the barriers keeping you
from being everything you're capable of being.

*Falling Together: How to Find Balance, Joy, and Meaningful
Change When Your Life Seems to be Falling Apart* by Donna
Cardillo. $16.95, 978-1-63152-077-8. A funny, big-hearted self-
help memoir that tackles divorce, caregiving, burnout, major
illness, fears, and low self-esteem—and explores the renewal that
comes when we are able to meet these challenges with courage.

*Tell Me Your Story: How Therapy Works to Awaken, Heal, and
Set You Free* by Tuya Pearl. $16.95, 978-1-63152-066-2. With
the perspective of both client and healer, this book moves you
through the stages of therapy, connecting body, mind, and spirit
with inner wisdom to reclaim and enjoy your most authentic life.

*The Clarity Effect: How Being More Present Can Transform Your
Work and Life* by Sarah Harvey Yao. $16.95, 978-1-63152-958-0.
A practical, strategy-filled guide for stressed professionals looking
for clarity, strength, and joy in their work and home lives.

Think Better. Live Better. 5 Steps to Create the Life You Deserve
by Francine Huss. $16.95, 978-1-938314-66-7. With the help of
this guide, readers will learn to cultivate more creative thoughts,
realign their mindset, and gain a new perspective on life.